Deconstructing Discrimination

Mirjam Holleman

May 2009
University College Roosevelt Academy,
International Honors College of Utrecht University at
Middelburg, the Netherlands

Introduction

Minority groups in America, as elsewhere in the world, have suffered much discrimination. America has known the Jim Crow laws that segregated African Americans from the white population. Today, laws that discriminate against homosexual people are under debate. Luckily, America has also witnessed significant social and institutional changes and inspiring leaders who gave their lives to bring about greater understanding and equality between disparate groups. *Deconstructing Discrimination* takes an anthropological, sociological, social psychological, and historical perspective to understand discrimination and the possibility of social and institutional change.

In cases where there is injustice and inequality, social change is important. A first step to perceiving how a situation or institution can change is to understand how that situation arose. How does one group of people become subordinated by and to another group? How do people start to differentiate between themselves and 'the other' so as to create these social categories – such as 'black' vs. 'white' person or 'homosexual' vs. 'heterosexual' person – in the first place? The construction of social systems of classification, which designate inclusion vs. exclusion, will be a major theme of this thesis.

Bringing about change in a society is a complex process. Deconstructing Discrimination examines the role played by individuals involved in the process of societal change. Individual dissenters become mobilized into mass movements. What reactions can be expected when a minority has set itself apart and pulls into question the social structures in which the majority feels comfortable? The dialectic between two competing paradigms that takes place in times of change can be observed throughout the chapter. Furthermore, the discourse of discrimination will be analyzed.

An important question of this thesis is: How can discriminatory practices and attitudes towards a particular, classified group of people eventually change? The first chapter will provide theories on the social construction of reality – including classification systems and identities – and how societies deal with differences and with change. The next two chapters will provide historical case examples of institutional and social change. The first of these chapters deals with the abolition of slavery in America. A specific focus on religious change will be taken. The final chapter of the thesis will focus on the current conflict about homosexuality in the church.

Content

Chapter 1 – Theory

Chapter 2 – The Abolition of Slavery

Chapter 3 – Gay Liberation

Deconstructing Discrimination – a Conclusion

Chapter 1 - Theory

Reality

Reality 101

To understand how accepted beliefs and/or social practices might be changed, it is first important to understand how people "get" their beliefs. Berger (de Jong, 2007) developed insightful theories regarding the social construction and institutionalization of reality. To explain this process, Berger introduced his concept of "the holy trinity of social construction" (de Jong, 2007, p. 347) which consists of three stages: externalization, objectivation, and internalization. Externalization refers to the need for humans to express their internal realities and share them with others. Through objectivation, social realities – such as norms and values- emerge and become observable in society. They are experienced as facts, "external to the producers" (de Jong, p. 347). Internalization then causes the individual who grows up in a certain social environment to accept and take for granted the reality that has been constructed by that society. Thus, reality is not an objective given, but is made to appear that way through continues social processes. De Jong (2007) explains that institutionalization occurs when "the group expects its members to conform" (p. 349) to certain habitualized patterns. Examples of institutionalized realities, habits, and customs include: languages, laws, marriage, and religious institutions. Reification occurs when institutions are no longer thought of as socially constructed phenomenon but are perceived as separate or transcendent from humanity. They are seen, for example, as natural facts or divine manifestations (de Jong, 2007). The danger of reification is that individuals accept without questioning - and do not see, or even consider looking for, possibilities for changing - institutions which may have lost their validity and/or function in society.

Classifications, Schemas, and Cognition

In one of her books, *How Institutions Think*, Douglas (1986) takes a deeper look into the influence of institutionalization on one's thoughts and perceptions. She argues that institutions create classifications and through them confer identities. Things are identified in their relation to other things with similar properties; these things are grouped together in one category or class. Douglas (1976) goes on to explain that during this process, things acquire names, which in turn influence the way they are perceived. Once labeled, something will be more easily fitted into one of the socially defined categories or schemas. Hence, it does not remain unidentified and unrecognized.

People's perceptions are schematic (Douglas, 1976). Multitudes of impressions reach ones senses, but what one perceives depends on what is recognizable according to one's cognitive schema and subconsciously classified as relevant. As an example of what ones world would be like without schemas, Aronson, et al (2007) describe a neurological disorder called Korsakov's Syndrome. People with Korsakov's Syndrome are unable to form new memories, and thus experience everything as if they are encountering it for the first time. They cannot place or "relate new experiences to ...past schemas" (Aronson et. al. p, 61). Schemas help us organize and make sense of perceptions, thus providing order, stability, and continuity in a world that might otherwise seem ambiguous, fragmented, and meaningless.

However, cognitive schemas are not universally the same for all people. One's cognitive schema is largely based one's culture and previous experiences. Aronson, Wilson, and Akert (2007) explain that through schemas, institutions"[instill] mental structures that influence the way we understand and interpret the world" (p. 71). Kuhn (McDonagh, 1976) presented the theory of paradigm. A paradigm can be defined as a "collective thought style" or "theoretical framework" (de Jong 2007, p.329) that guides people's observations and interpretations. Kuhn theorized that scientists, for example, work within a particular paradigm that tells them what to investigate and guides their research. A paradigm thus influences how things are looked at and the questions that are raised, but the paradigm itself is not usually looked at or questioned. In sum, schemas are useful, even necessary, but it does remain important to remember that they are socially constructed and thus neither static nor substantive.

Classifications Confer Identity

Moreover, "comparisons of cultures make it clear that no superficial sameness of properties explains how items [whether it's people or things] get assigned to classes. Everything depends on which properties are selected" (Douglas, 1986, p. 58). Without knowledge of the institution's paradigm, or collective thought style, one would not recognize the sameness in the items commonly grouped together by that institution. For example, the Bible book Leviticus groups together the camel, the hare, the pig, and the rock badger and labels them as 'impure' animals -each of them happens to be unclassifiable as a cloven hoofed, cud chewing ungulate – having only one but not both characteristics (Douglas, 1976, p.56) - but these animals appear to have nothing in common to one who is not familiar with the specific classification system or criteria being used. This has led to the common assumption that certain animals were arbitrarily labeled as 'impure' by the Leviticans, whilst other scholars searched for inherent qualities in each of the animals in question to provide a medical or hygiene related explanation for it being labeled impure. Douglas (1999) argued against both these lines of thought. The label, she pointed out, says almost nothing about the animal itself, but can only be understood by – and simultaneously be analyzed to gain a greater understanding of - the larger social order or system that was used to classify it. Sameness, as well as identity, is thus "conferred upon elements within a coherent scheme" (Douglas, 1986, p. 59). It is not inherent or substantive. An identity is socially constructed and relationally constituted according to the institutions criteria.

A Social Reality Based on Constructed Classifications

Berger's concept of reification occurs to classifications when "sets of similar things are so well-established within a particular culture that their sameness has the authority of self-evidence" (Douglas 1986, p. 60). Take for example gender classifications in the western world. It appears to us self-evident that there are two genders – male and female. All males are male to us, and all females female; while some other cultures acknowledge more than two possible genders (Parker, 2001).

Douglas (1986) adds that as labels are being invented to identify certain 'groups' of people, these people readily come to accept and identify themselves as that label. Thus people build institutions, "and the institutions make new labels, and the label makes new kinds of people" (p, 108). Institutions not only make salient some personal characteristics by grouping and labeling them (e.g. male, female), they also determine which aspects are considered more defining for one's identity than others. For instance in some cultures a person's place of origin says the most about their identity, while in other societies one's occupation is most defining. The salience of certain accepted identity categories can also diminish, grow stronger, or be overshadowed by another over time in one society.

A Dialectic Process

Douglas (1986) appeals for the recognition of institutional influences on individual cognition, but also wishes to point out the individual's role in institution-building. She (1976) makes clear that the individual, as part of a social system, is not merely a passive recipient and adherent of its institutions - such as its language – but, often unintentionally and unknowingly, contributes to changes in these institutions. This view on the individual's role in the social construction of reality is expanded by social psychologist Solomon Asch.

Asch (Levine, 1999), has stated that individuals, as social beings, are engaged in "cooperative efforts to understand the world" (p. 360). He sees the process as an exchange between independence on the one hand, and conformity on the other. Individuals need to express their own perspectives and experiences - this requires independence - but also should consider others' viewpoints and possible alter their own – conformity. Groups have a tendency to reach a consensus and thus construct a shared, social reality. Although Asch (Levine, 1999) saw this process as "natural" and "rational" and even described it as "a dynamic requirement of the situation" (p. 360), he made clear that the consensus reached by the group is not always valid. For this reason, independence should persistently play a crucial role in the construction of social reality. An individual should "adhere to the testimony of his experience and steadfastly maintain his hold on reality" (Asch 1952, p. 360).

Thus, while Berger focused on the individual's view of reality as an internalization of the reality constructed by his social environment, the individual in Asch's view seemingly has more space to 'look outside the box,' perceive things differently, and influence the group. Moreover, although Berger acknowledged that the individual certainly plays a part in the social construction of reality (de Jong, 2007), Asch went another step further and indicated that the individual has a certain *responsibility* in the construction process (Levine, 1999). As Levine (1999) puts it, "conformity is socially useful only if it is based on independence" (p. 360).

Douglas (1986) underscores the importance of intellectual independence, explaining that: "the necessary first step in resistance is to discover how the institutional grip is laid upon our mind" (p. 92). Here she refers to sociologist Robert K. Merton's back-door approach to the self-referencing dilemma. For instance, one could ask oneself how one is prevented from thinking, specifically about the constraints placed on one's thoughts by the institution one is a part of. "What are the impossible thoughts?" (p. 76) and why do these thoughts seem impossible to a member of this institution? In order to optimize one's individualism, and potentially enhance the functioning of one's institutions, Douglas agrees with Merton that, "we need a technique for standing aside from our own society" (Douglas p. 75). If an individual detects a flaw in the collective way of thinking, or is not in agreement with an institution, Asch (Levine, 1999) would say he or she has the responsibility to speak up in order to fine-tune social reality. But how will the members of a group react towards an individual or minority group that points out the faults of the majority and refuses to conform?

Reactions

To better understand the reactions of the group specifically towards a nonconforming individual, it is important to first discuss anthropological and sociological theories on how societies deal with differences and/or change in general.

The Hardiness of an Institution's Paradigm

Douglas (1986) exemplifies the role of an institution's paradigm on an individual's perceptions, thoughts, and emotions by highlighting modern scientists' stubborn ignorance of, and resistance to, the incidence of multiple discoveries of the same thing. She refers to Merton's publications: "Priorities in Scientific Discovery" (1957), "Singletons and Multiples in Scientific Discovery" (1962), and "Resistance to the Study of Multiple Discoveries in Science" (1963). Multiple discoveries are a known phenomenon occurring when scientific discoveries were not acknowledged by the society in which they first appeared - because the society's paradigm either offered too much resistance or simply could not perceive the significance of the discovery at the time - but 'when the time was ripe,' so to speak, these previously rejected ideas resurfaced and came to be labeled as new discoveries. Douglas aptly summarizes Merton's research on scientists' reactions to evidence of previous discoveries of 'their' discovery:

> The analysis shows that the star scientist, normally benign and generous, furiously deny a convergent or earlier discovery because their passions are driven by the way that science is organized. Merton links emotion, cognition, and social structure into one system. In science, the big rewards go to accredited innovations. The concept of original discovery is embedded in all forms of institutional life, along with prizes and naming of plants, animals, measurements, and even diseases after scientists. [...] Using Freudian terms, he defined the resistance as motivated denial of an accessible but painful reality. (p. 75).

Douglas (1986) sums up the influence of institutions by saying they "systematically direct individual memory and channel our perceptions into forms compatible with the relations they authorize. They fix processes that are essentially dynamic, they hide their influence, and they rouse our emotions to a standardized pitch on standardized issues" (p. 92).

Social psychological research moreover affirms the endurance of schemas, even after these have been proved false. "Schemas can take on a life of their own, even after the evidence for them has been completely discredited" (Aronson, et al. 2007, p. 66). This "perseverance effect" (Aronson, et al. 2007) was discovered in an experiment in which participants were asked to read through a stack of (all fictitious) suicide notes. The participants were told that some of them were real, whilst others were fictitious. They were asked to determine which were false and which were real. They were given immediate feedback by the experimenter as they stated their guess for each note. Half of the participants were given the feedback that their guess was right for 24 of the 25 notes – thus leading the participant to believe that he or she was remarkably good at this task. After the 25th card however, the experimenter told the participant that he or she had been assigned to a condition in which the participant would be told he or she was correct 24 times, regardless of how well he or she actually did. Next, the participant was asked to guess how many answers he or she *actually* got correct.

Conversely, the other half of the participants in the experiment were led to believe that they got many answers wrong, were then told that they had been assigned to a condition where they would be told they were wrong most of the time, and were then asked to guess how many of their answers they thought were *actually* correct. Although all participants understood that the experimenter's feedback had been staged (though they did not know that all of the suicide notes were in fact fake, too) the participants' estimation of how many times they thought they guessed correctly regarding the authenticity of the suicide notes was significantly higher for those who had been given "success" feedback than for participants that initially receive "failure" feedback. Cognitive schemas or beliefs, once implanted in our minds, are not easily changed, even when confronted with reliable, opposing information.

Defining Dirt and Danger

Douglas investigated reactions to 'differences' in her book *Purity and Danger* (1976). Here she described society as continuously watchful against internal and external threats. Anything that does not belong in, or does not comply with the 'natural' laws of the society stands in opposition to it and is a potential danger. Often it is these things that are labeled as 'unclean.' She famously stated that "dirt is matter out of place" (Lambek, 2007, p. 194) or something outside of a constituted order. She observes the coherence between a society's ideas and definitions of uncleanliness and its general social order, but makes clear that these ideas and definitions are not static but, like the social system itself, can and do change. She asserts that ideas about uncleanliness are relationally constituted and they symbolically express social systems. Since 'dirt' cannot be substantively defined or seen as an isolated phenomenon, one society's views about 'purity and danger' cannot be evaluated as more correct than another's.

Dealing with Anomalies

As noted in the previous section about the social construction of reality, all societies use classification systems in order to construct reality and explain the world around them. Ambiguous impressions will be interpreted to fit an individual's cognitive schema, which is based on the social system. That which disrupts the established order will be ignored or dealt with in another way. Douglas used the term anomaly to refer to that which does not fit into any of the socially established categories of identification. She (1999) defined her theory of anomaly as "a universal feeling of disquiet (even of disgust) on confrontation with unclassifiables" (p. vii). Ones behavior towards an anomaly is a reaction to the fact that something has challenged or confused ones trusted classification system. From her anthropological observations and research Douglas (1976) outlines and exemplifies five negative ways in which societies cope with anomalies:

1. Redefining: When a handicapped baby is born to the Nuer of Southern Sudan, it is said to be a hippopotamus, accidentally born to humans, and laid in the water where it is presumed to belong.

2. Extermination: The birth of twins threatens the Ibo of Nigeria's social classification that all humans give birth to singletons. Twins were left to die, and their mother would be expelled from the village. Another example comes from societies where cocks are classified as birds that crow at dawn; night-crowing cocks have their necks wrung.

3. Avoidance: In the Bible book of Leviticus, rules prohibited contact with 'crawling things' as these could not be classified in the categories of edible game, fowl, or fish. Moreover, Michel Foucault (see Bowie, 2006), in his work *Madness and Civilization,* recounts that, in the past, the primary function of mental institutions was to keep deviant people away from the public social sphere.

4. Labeling as dangerous: stigmatization and/or persecution has been the fate of many deviant individuals or groups. For example, followers of the Craft (witches) are often falsely accused of being Satanists and/or child abusers.

5. Incorporating into Ritual: For example, rituals surrounding death can situate death in a greater scheme of things, portraying it as a new form of existence, for instance.

Keep in mind that - although most of the examples above refer to anomalous people or animals-ideas, beliefs, or behaviors can also be seen as anomalous and be confronted as such. Moreover, Douglas makes clear that anomalies do not necessarily have to be dealt with in a *negative* way. They can also be dealt with positively. This occurs when they are, first of all, acknowledged and later accommodated into an adjusted paradigm or view on reality.

Researching the Root of Resentment and Rejection

Monin, Sawyer, and Marquez (2008) recount numerous documentations of moral rebels - defined as "individuals who take a principled stand against the status quo, who refuse to comply, stay silent, or simply go along when this would require that they compromise their values" (p. 76) - and whistleblowers who consequently suffered under the hostile reactions of their peers, ranging from rejection to death-threats and outright violence. According to Monin et al. (2008) the rejection of 'moral rebels' is not due to a general social disproval of such behavior. In fact, these individuals are often viewed as heroes by outsiders who are not, or no longer, involved in the situation. Think of Martin Luther King or Mahatma Gandhi, for example. It is socially admirable to be an independent-thinker and to hold on to your moral convictions despite fierce opposition. Why are moral rebels consistently rejected by members of their own society, then? One might assume that, especially in the case of whistleblowers, rejection could be a rational reaction of those members in the group who might suffer consequences from the rebel's actions. However, Monin et al. (2008) provide the example of Joseph Darby, the man who reported the Abu Ghraib abuses and later received serious threats from former colleagues, to illustrate that "rejection does not just come from peers who stand to suffer from the rebellion, but also from peers who merely failed to report or oppose the abuse" (p. 76). Another example of this phenomenon is provided by a variation to Milgram's (1965) famous experiment on obedience to authority.

In the original version of the experiment (Milgram, 1976), which was cunningly presented as an experiment into the effects of punishment on learning, the volunteers were divided into 'learner' and 'teacher' pairs. Unbeknown to the real volunteers, those who were - supposedly randomly - assigned the role of the learners were actors and accomplices of Milgram. The 'teacher' (real volunteer) was then placed behind a switchboard with 30 voltage levels, ranging from 15 to 450 volts. These voltage levels were also marked with words indicating the severity of the shock, ranging from "Slight Shock" to "Danger: Severe Shock." The teacher was then instructed to read a series of questions to the learner, to administer an electric shock to the learner each time he answered incorrectly, and to increase the voltage level by one increment every time. The shock generator was of course fake and would not cause real harm or discomfort to the 'learner.' Throughout the experiment, however, the 'teacher' was under the impression that he was administering real, increasingly more severe, electric shocks to the learner. Nobody could have predicted the shocking results of this experiment: 62.5% of all participants went through with the experiment until the very end, administering the most severe, 450-volt, electric shock. At debriefing, the majority of subjects expressed deep regret and bewilderment at their own behavior during the experiment.

In a variation to this experiment, Milgram (1965) introduced a 'moral rebel' who refused to go along with the experiment. This adaptation provided interesting opportunities to observe insiders' reactions towards a rebel in their midst. At debriefing, participants who had kept shocking the victim displayed a rejecting attitude towards the rebels. Rebels were judged as whiners who "were just being ridiculous" and "lost all control of themselves" (Milgram 1965, study 2, p. 132). While outsiders reading about the experiment would surely take the side of the moral rebel and praise him for his courage and altruism, those involved in the experiment made complaints like, "They (the rebel) came here to do the experiment, and I think they should have stuck with it" (Milgram 1965, study 2, p. 132).

It is remarkable to note that the subjects who went through with Milgram's experiment on their own (not exposed to a moral rebel) later expressed regret - which illustrates that most people do judge the actions required by the experiment as morally wrong - and wished they had had the courage to rebel; while those who went through with the experiment despite the objections of a moral rebel later justified their own actions and criticized rebellion. As Monin et al. (2008) noted, "the exact same behavior can be constructed in such different ways depending on the perceiver's involvement" (p. 77). Merton (1957) also noted this phenomenon when he referred to the sociologist Robert Young's saying "in-group virtues become out-group vices" (p. 426) meaning that the same behavior that is judged as admirable when performed by members of the in-group, is somehow interpreted differently and criticized when it applies to members of the out-group. In Milgram's experiment, the subjects would have judged rebellion as admirable if they themselves had had the courage to do it, but judged someone else's rebellion as objectionable when they themselves continued with the experiment. "Is the in-group hero frugal, thrifty, and sparing? Then the out-group villain is stingy, miserly and penny-pinching" (Merton, p. 428). It can be concluded, then, that a group's rejection of a moral rebel has little to do with the action in question - for example, whether it is right or wrong to shock an innocent victim. Or whether nonconformity, on the grounds of moral objections, is praiseworthy or deplorable - but probably has more to do with deeper psychological processes of the actors involved in a social situation.

Monin et al. (2008) set out to discover "the root of resentment" towards moral rebels (p. 77). Recall Berger's theories on the social construction of reality, described in the first section of this paper. One's identity is also largely socially constructed according to Berger (de Jong, 2007; Cooper, 1990). One may hold a certain image of oneself, but if others do not affirm this image, one will generally reconsider its reality. People are continually looking for confirmation of who they believe they are. Monin et al. (2008) suggest that, through nonconformity, the rebel implicitly pulls into question the behavior of conforming members of the group and "shakes the perceivers confidence in being a good, moral person" (p. 77). If the self is socially constructed, than self-esteem is dependent on the - explicit or implicit - affirmation of others. Since morality is central to most people's self-concept (Allison, Messick, & Goethals, 1989; See Monin et al.), the socio-psychological threat caused by the rebel can be severe and lead to defensive behavior and attacks from the group.

Through a series of ingenious experiments, Monin et al. (2008) were able to show the validity of their hypothesis that:
- Reproach, even imagined, shakes actors' overall sense of self-worth.
- The rejection of rebels would be an attempt to deny this vulnerability and to preserve one's sense of being a good person.

- If this is true, then individuals who have been secured in their moral and adaptive adequacy, this is, self-affirmed (Steele, 1988), should show less need to reject rebels or deny the implications of their stance (p. 78).

The perceived vulnerability to the self-image of the conforming person is more than a rational psychological consequence of being confronted with someone who behaved 'more morally' than oneself. Monin et al. (2008) discovered that the observed vulnerability to conformists' self-worth, and the subsequent resentment of moral rebels, could not have been caused by the fact that "rebels make individuals less happy with their own decision or that rebels make individuals more aware that they could have gone beyond the pressure of the situation" (p. 84), as this was not found to be the case, neither in Monin et al.'s experiment, nor in Milgram's experiment discussed earlier. On the contrary: The moral rebels' opposing stance was likely to make individuals defend and justify their own actions all the more (Monin et al., 2008; Milgram, 1965).

Monin et al. (2008) then theorized that conforming actors in a social situation imagine the disproval of a nonconformist towards them and implicitly feel rejected by him or her – this sense of rejection causes the conformist to feel vulnerable in his or her self-worth. To reduce this vulnerability, conformists preemptively reject the rebel. The results of Monin et al. first set of experiments showed that imagined rejection indeed played a significant role in the conformers' rejection of moral-rebels. As this fear of rejection prevailed despite the fact that the experiment was set up so that the moral rebel and conformer would never actually meet each other, it was concluded that "imagined rejection may be less a threat to an actual social relationship than a threat to one's personal sense of integrity and self-worth" (p. 84).

After this was concluded, Monin et al. (2008) set out to further test their theories and made two predictions: 1) "Self-affirmation opens the heart" and 2) "self-affirmation opens the eyes," meaning that 1) individuals who feel confident in their self-worth will be less likely to reject moral rebels, despite the fact that these self-confident individuals may still believe that the moral-rebel would dislike them, and 2) self-affirmed individuals will be more open to the moral rebels point-of-view and more willing to admit their own mistakes. To find out if these predictions could be validated, Monin et al. manipulated feelings of self-worth of half of the participants by asking them to reflect on, and write about, "a recent experience in which you demonstrated a quality or value that is very important to you and which made you feel good about yourself" (p. 85), before subjecting them to the actual experiment in which they would be confronted either with a rebel who expressed moral objections to the experiment, or an obedient other. Monin et al. found that, although self-affirmed, conforming participants "knew that rebels would probably not hold them in high regard" (p. 88), this did not negatively affect their evaluation of the rebels. Moreover:

> Self-affirmed individuals were better able to give credit when credit was due...they saw the rebel as particularly moral and agentic, reported being less happy with their own choice than participants observing an obedient other, and even saw that they might not have been as constrained by the situation as they thought at the time (Monin et al. 2008, p. 88).

These findings might provide important clues as to how an individual can effectively bring about social change.

Restructuring

When and why is nonconformity or rebelliousness required? And will nonconformists always face unrelenting resistance from the majority? If this were the case, social change would not be possible. People would forever adhere to the status quo of the established social reality, rebels would be immediately rejected, and society would remain static. History teaches us that this is not the case. Societies do change. How institutions change – and the dialectic between the old and the new 'reality' during the transition process - will be the focus of this thesis. This thesis will present two documentations and analyses of social/institutional change in the U.S., applying the previously discussed theory and research.

The first of these analyses concerns the Abolition Movement of the 19th century. It will document the history of slavery in the Americas to discover how it became institutionalized - how it became a structural part of social reality, and justified and reified in the minds of individual slaveholders. Next, it will explore how social movements and tension can lead to societal change. The role of the individual in this process will be presented using Abraham Lincoln as a case example. The chapter will also discuss how the enslavement of African people by Europeans in the Americas led to new ways of classifying and identifying people based on their skin color. This processes is significant in how we view the discrimination against the differentiated and subordinated 'black' people.

The next chapter looks at the current conflict of homosexuality and the church as an example of a 'paradigm shift' in process. Specific discourses on conservative Christian websites will be analyzed using Douglas' (1986) anthropological observations on how a culture that adheres to a certain paradigm or 'collective thought style' deals with anomalies. An attempt will be made to discover what led to the discrimination towards homosexual people in modern society. If the institution of slavery led to the construction of race, what led to the social construction of homosexuality? This question cannot be answered with any degree of certainty, but theories pertaining to modernization and the organization of social and family life in a capitalist society will be provided. Finally, the beginnings of the on-going gay liberation movement will be documented and compared to the civil rights movement of the 1960s in which black people in America finally attained equal rights to white people.

Chapter 2 - The Abolition of Slavery

Slavery in the Americas

Colonialism and the reintroduction of slavery

Slavery was a common phenomenon in many societies of the world, until the rise of Christianity (Wesley, 1774; Stark, 2004). The institution began to lose its grip in about the 8th century in Spain and slavery was discontinued in most European societies from then on. Wesley (1774) claims that it remained an extinct practice for Europeans until the sixteenth century with the discovery of the Americas (p. 5). Slavery thus became reinstituted in the Americas as one of the many consequence of colonialism.

With the discovery of the Americas, countries such as Spain, Portugal, and England set up colonies and plantations to detract valuable products such as cotton, sugar, and tobacco from these lands. Each colonizing country was in a race against the others to secure the best land and make the most profit of it to benefit its kingdom (Blackburn, 1988; Tignor, Adelman, Aron, Brown, Elman, Kotkin, Lui, Merchand, Pittman, Prakash, Shaw, & Tsin, 2008). Traders thus entered the Americas with this goal in mind; they were not there to settle in the new land, but simply to extract the most resources from it and transport these back to their own country.

Unfamiliar with the qualities of the new found land and the harsher climates, colonists first relied on the labor of the natives too make a profit. However, as natives began to die out due to warfare and diseases introduced by the colonists, a new solution had to be found. The first African slaves were imported into Hispaniola by Spanish colonists in 1508 (Wesley, 1774). Thus, slavery became reinstituted in the New World.

Gradual institutionalization of slavery

Both Morgan (1975) and Peabody & Grinberg (2007) describe the process towards institutionalized slavery in Virginia, one of the main colonies of England, as gradual and not entirely deliberate: "Negro slavery came to America without anyone having to decide upon it as a matter of public policy" (Morgan, p. 330), "The English had no expectation or policy to rely on slave laboring America" (Peabody & Grinberg, p. 11). Noel (1972b) also attests that "Slavery was not established by law in any American colony, but its development by custom was later recognized by legislation" (p. 166). Someone did not suddenly decide to institutionalize slavery, thinking it would be economically advantageous and ignoring all moral objections. It was more or less contingently built into the forming society of the Americas.

As mentioned earlier, colonists needed a strong labor force to work their plantations. The English first relied on servants. The system of servanthood helped put England's poor and unemployed to work and it of course empowered and profited the rich who were able to afford servants. When slaves became available, and for various reasons also more profitable than regular servants, by the year 1660, "Virginians had only to buy men who were already enslaved… They converted to slavery simply by buying slaves instead of servants" (Morgan p. 297). The fact that they did not have to enslave anyone themselves lessened the cognitive dissonance of an act that might otherwise have been seen as immoral. Myths surrounding the morality of slavery served to further justify these transactions. For instance, it was commonly claimed that slavery was beneficial for the African savage as it transported him from his barbaric homeland and allowed him opportunities (education, religion, etc.) to be transformed into a civilized human being (Tise, 1987; d'Anjou, 1996): "The South has advanced the Africans, as a whole, more rapidly than any other low savage race has ever been educated" (Dabney, 1867, p. 216). Where did these myths come from? To answer this question, one will need to consider "…the resemblance between servants and slaves in the plantation system and in the consciousness of those who ran it" (Morgan, p. 316).

From Servanthood to Slavery

It is important to understand the English's work ethic during this time in history. Poverty was a major social problem in England, especially in cities such as London. Morgan (1975) describes London, through the eyes of an English statesmen at the time, as an overpopulated, impoverished city full of lazy drunkards and uneducated, unemployed beggars and thieves. What accounted for this misery? Why was England not making advances like other European countries, English statesmen and economists asked themselves? The poor were blamed for the disjointed condition of the city. They were despised for their laziness, for leading London to ruin and making it almost unlivable. They needed to be dealt with and usefully employed. Systems and institutions of involuntary servanthood arose to "extract the maximum labor from them" (p. 321) so that the poor could be a source of wealth rather than burden. After 1660, "workhouses" sprang up around England; Foucault has termed this movement "the great confinement" (Morgan, 1975, p. 321). England's upper-class viewed these institutions as a great success and necessity. At workhouses, 'the poor' were kept off the streets where they were nothing but a nuisance to 'civilized' Londoners; they were usefully employed, contributing to the wealth of the nation; and they and their children were conditioned in the important habit of work, rather than laziness. At workhouses, the poor could be tolerated, even appreciated, by their society. Hence rose the association between work, civilization, and human worth.

Perhaps it was the local success of enforced labor that made the English eager to apply this ethic in the New World and begin imposing it on the uncivilized 'other.' "Christopher Carleill…reported how good-for-nothing English beggars had become new men when given a job to do in the English army in the Netherlands. If such paupers were shipped to North America, they would surely have more to do and a better life than in the army. Similarly, the Indians, who now eked out a savage existence without proper clothing or housing, would be transformed by the material comforts of civilization and the spiritual comforts of Christianity" (Morgan, 1975, p. 22). With this Utopia in mind, the English set out convincing themselves they were doing everyone a favor. As American Indians died out, and English servants became nearly impossible to maintain, the English colonists shifted their 'experiment' and their ethics to African slaves. Their methods of 'helping' the unemployed and the savage alike conveniently provided the initial justifications for the institutionalization of slavery.

Not only were African slaves treated the same as European poor, they were also perceived practically the same way. Slaves, at first, were simply "the labor force of a plantation much as servants had been" (Morgan, 1975, p. 319). Comparing historical documents, such as letters, in which wealthy plantation owners wrote about their servants or slaves, Morgan (1975) observes that "Both [servants and slaves, in the eyes of their respective masters] displayed the same attitude and habits: they were shiftless, irresponsible, unfaithful, ungrateful, dishonest; they got drunk whenever possible; they did not work hard enough or regularly enough" (p. 319). In this way, the English's attitude towards their poor became superimposed on the black slave. "The contempt that lay behind …many of the workhouse schemes is not easy to distinguish from the kind of contempt that today we call racism" (Morgan, 1975, p. 325). A more detailed explanation of the development of slavery will be provided later on in this paper.

Why the Africans became the slaves

Now that the similarities between English servants and African slaves have been presented, the question arises: What made the Africans, as a social category, different from poor

European immigrants? Europeans were never turned into slaves, even though their status was at first very similar to that of the Africans. "In the seventeenth century many immigrants in addition to the Africans – Swedes, Armenians, Jews – had brought no family names to America. By the eighteenth all but the Negroes had acquired them" (Handlin, 1972, p. 33). Poor Europeans avoided becoming slaves and collectively improved their status in the Americas over time, while the Africans' status of slave seemed to become increasingly more consolidated. What accounted for this divergence of fates?

Some might argue that it was racism that made Africans into slaves of the Europeans. An underlying positive prejudice towards white people would have prevented European planters from enslaving 'their own kind'. However, "judging from the very nasty treatment suffered by white indentured servants, it was obviously not sentiment which prevented the Virginia planters from enslaving their fellow Englishman" (Harris, p. 69, quoted in Noel 1972 p. 120). Noel would argue that it was their circumstances, not their color, that allowed Africans to be turned into slaves in the Americas.

Noel (1972c) explains that white indentured servants had more power and effective spokesmen to prevent being turned into slaves. Moreover, Africans were more likely than the European servants to be in the Americas against their will. Being far from their homeland, their tribe and community, lacking a common language to communicate with the strangers around them – being, essentially, alone –African slaves were exceptionally vulnerable to persistent exploitation. Noel (1972) also explains that the lack of unity in the Negro community further contributed to their lack of power and agency in the Americas around the 17th century. African slaves were made into a distinct social category, but they did not at first see themselves as such. There was no sense of "we" - the black people, the Africans – among them. "The absence of a shared identification among seventeenth century Negroes reflected the absence of a shared heritage from which to construct identity, draw strength, and organize protest" (Noel, p. 120). Africans were alone in the Americas. They lacked the group solidarity that would centuries later provide them with a powerful agency to change the social order and their place within it. They could not escape slavery, because who would they join? Unlike Native Americans – who were also culturally diverse before European colonization, but developed a sufficient sense of shared heritage to support and protect each other against the white men (Noel, 1972, p. 121) – Africans could not join forces with members of their own group, because this group identity did not yet exist. By the time this sense of shared identity did develop, the social order with its unequal balance of power between white vs. black people in America already seemed fixed and change could barely be negotiated.

Beginnings of Abolition

Blackburn (1988) explains that, although there were undoubtedly certain independent-thinking individuals in the late seventeenth and early eighteenth century who disagreed with the morality of slavery, true protests were rare. The institution of slavery had become so entrenched in the social, economic, and moral world of the colonies that rejecting it remained nothing but a private matter of opinion. Moreover, it is important to realize that most of these private protests did not even reject the institution of slavery at its root, but only abhorred the way it was being executed. For to truly reject the whole concept of slavery at this time meant to reject an entire social order and the way life was organized. Peabody & Grinberg (2007) also comment on the in fact "peculiar idea" (p.11) of abolition, as slavery had been viewed as a historically and morally normal institution until the beginning of the abolition movement. Therefore, "philosophical attacks on New World slavery – that is to say on the institution itself rather than on cruel excesses of particular masters or traders – were extremely rare prior to the middle of the eighteenth century" (Blackburn, p. 36).

Religious Roots of the Abolition Movement

However, a group of like-minded abolitionist, namely the Quakers, on religious-moral grounds (Peabody & Grinberg, 2007; d'Anjou, 1996; Blackburn, 1988), did oppose the institution of slavery at a Pennsylvania Meeting in 1688: "The Germantown petition comes closest of all the early protests to making out a radical case against slavery" (Blackburn, 1988, p. 44)

> There is a saying that we should doe to all men like as we will be done ourselves; making no difference of what generation, descent or colour they are. And those who steal or rob men, and those who buy or purchase them, are they not all alike? Here is liberty of conscience, wch is right and reasonable; here ought to be likewise liberty of ye body, except of ye evil-doers which is another case. But to bring men hither and to rob or sell them against their will, we stand against. In Europe there are many oppressed for conscience sake; and here there are those oppressed who are of a black colour... this makes an ill report in all countries of Europe, where they here off, that ye Quakers doe here handel men as they handel there ye cattle... if once these slaves (wch they say are so

wicked and stubborn men) should joint themselves – fight for their freedom – and handel
their masters and mistresses as they did handel them before; will these masters and
mistresses take the sword at hand and warr against these poor slaves… (p. 45).
Although clearly pro-abolitionist, this petition did not reach a wide public. D'Anjou (1996) says

that although the Quakers were "[undertaking] collective action against slavery and the slave

trade…they acted more as a pressure group than as a social movement" (p. 147). Blackburn

(1988) outlines a few more of these kinds of "isolated and sporadic protests" (p. 46). Moreover,

Blackburn mentions violent slave revolts, which "could coalesce into a general attack on the

slaveholder regime, while still not formally challenging the juridical institution of slavery" (p.

56). Such small-scale forms of resistance as just described thus did not pose a threat to the social

system of slavery.

Slavery, like any other kind of institution, was not an isolated phenomenon. It formed a

part of a larger social system. The entire social order needed to be shaken and challenged –

"putting in question the organizing principles of power" (Blackburn, p. 58) - before any real

change could be brought about. It would take more than a few individual protestors; more than a

few united individuals with a common cause against slavery. "Fundamental ideological shifts in

a society do not merely happen without reference to historical events" (Tise, 1987, p. 191). War,

combined with a resurgence of Christian movements, played a big part towards this effect. The

first of these wars was the American Revolutionary War (1775-1783). However, this paper will

not discuss the events of this war as it does not seem relevant to the focus of this thesis. What is

significant is that, after the war, true manumission societies began to arise (Blackburn, 1988).

D'Anjou (1996), Blackburn (1988), and Peabody & Grinberg (2007) highlight the

significance of the Christian Evangelical movement as a catalyst towards the true abolition of

slavery. For example "The spread of Methodism in the US South in the 1780s…showed a latent

animosity to slaveholders which was hidden in stable periods" (Blackburn, p. 525). Later, the

American Civil War (1861-1865), which will be discussed in the next section about Abraham

Lincoln, legitimized the cause of the abolitionist, It seems that the tension of war - or the general

social unrest and instability associated with it – was needed to bring sentiments against slavery to

the fore in society, and put slavery on the table as a pertinent social issue to be dealt with.

The Individual – Abraham Lincoln

Abraham Lincoln, the 16th president of the United States, led the country through the Civil War (1861-1865), preserving the Union and abolishing slavery. In the presidential election campaign of 1860, Abraham Lincoln and his party, the Republicans, promised to put an end to the expansion of slavery beyond the states where the institution already existed. Because of this, when Lincoln was voted president, seven Southern slaveholding states announced their secession from the Union and called themselves the Confederate States of America. Thus began the Civil War. In 1862, Lincoln signed the Emancipation Declaration that made the abolition of slavery the main goal of the continuing Civil War (Franklin, 2000). In the history books and the minds of Americans and the world alike, Lincoln is remembered for his great, political influence that led to the abolition of slavery. But who was this man? What were his views? How were they shaped by his society and his position within it? Did he display the power of independent thought and take on the responsibility of nonconforming action? Was he able to impact the social order of his society?

Lincolns views on slavery were certainly influenced by the structure of the society in which he lived and his place within that social order. Although his views were quite progressive at the time, and he wished he could abolish slavery and free the slaves, he only saw one possible mode of action: freed slaves would have to be transplanted to Liberia (Howard, 1999) or colonies in Central America (Lincoln, 1862). Lincoln could not envision the black person in American society, other than as a slave. He declared "we can not…make them equal" (Lincoln, Oct. 16, 1854. Quoted in Howard, 1999, p. 30). This statement was not based on some kind of moral opinion - that it would be wrong to make blacks equal to whites - rather, it just seemed like a self-evident impossibility to Lincoln given the circumstances of his society. "My own feelings will not admit of this; and if mine would, we well know that those of the great mass of white people will not…[and] a universal feeling, whether well or ill-founded, can not be safely disregarded" (Lincoln, Oct. 16, 1854. Quoted in Howard, 1999, p. 30). This constitutes a clear example of what Merton (see Douglas, 1986) meant with his notions of "impossible thoughts," which point to the constraints placed on an individual's thoughts by the institution's paradigm. Lincoln's views were constrained by the prevailing reality of the society in which he lived.

The first speeches and writings of Lincoln (Baker, 2000; Howard, 1999) show that he personally agreed with the abolitionists and viewed slaver as wrong, however, as a politician he had to also consider the will of the large number of slaveholders in the States. The title of the first chapter of Howard (1999) sums up the dilemma: " Lincoln on Slavery: A Constitutional Right and a Moral Wrong" (p. 19). Baker (2000) observes that at the beginning of his political career, in the Illinois legislature, "the young Lincoln gave few signs that he would one day be the man who freed the slaves" (p. 58). The following document was signed by Lincoln on March 3, 1837.

> Resolution upon the subject of domestic slavery having passed both branches of the General Assembly at its present session, the undersigned hereby protest against the passage of the same.
> They believe that the institution of slavery is founded on both injustice and bad policy; but that the promulgation of abolition doctrines tends rather to increase than to abate its evils.
> They believe that the Congress of the United States has no power, under the constitution, to interfere with the institution of slavery in the different states.
> They believe that the Congress of the United States has the power, under the constitution, to abolish slavery in the District of Columbia; butt that that power ought not to be exercised unless at the requestof the people of said District.
> The difference between these opinions and those contained in the said resolutions, is their reason for entering this protest.
> Dan Stone,
> A. Lincoln,
> Representatives from the county of Sangamon. (Baker, 2000, p. 58).

As a president, Lincoln was put in the position of main representative and leader of the system; making radical changes to the system would get him into trouble. Therefore, he originally proposed "a natural death" of slavery (Howard, 1999, p. 24). Lincoln felt wary of making any radical changes, preferring rather to proceed cautiously and thoughtfully. He was thus in a sense restricted, rather than empowered to take action, by his position as a political leader in society.

Two conflicting goals were at play: unifying the states and abolishing slavery. At first it seemed these two goals could not support each other, thus compromising Lincolns scope of agency. However, he skillfully found a way to make the abolition of slavery conducive towards fighting for the Union of the States – this was expressed in the Emancipation Proclamation. The Emancipation Proclamation freed African slaves to join the civil war, fighting for their own freedom *and* the preservation of the Union. Franklin (2000) describes the writing and issuing of the Emancipation Proclamation as a big step for Lincoln, because "Unlike Jefferson, whose Declaration of Independence was a clean break with a legal and constitutional system that had hitherto restricted thought and action, Lincoln was compelled to forge a document of freedom for the slaves within the existing constitutional system in a manner that would give even greater support to that constitutional system" (p. 87).

How did Lincoln resolve the divisive issue of slavery? Initially, Howard (1999) notes, Lincoln hoped to change people's attitudes towards slavery, which would eventually lead the institution towards extinction. However, in time, it became evident that the crucial step towards ending slavery was not a change of minds but a change in the way society was ordered and structured. "[destroying] their antebellum world…and constructing an improved Union" (Howard 1999, p. 24), through civil war, became the primary means to abolish slavery. As one will notice in the following section, the institution of slavery had become so embedded the society, the lives, and the minds of the slaveholders – it was such a structural part of their reality - that they were capable of providing rational, and at the time very persuasive, arguments to defend the system.

Anti-Abolitionist Arguments

The following section of this paper will focus on a book from 1867 entitled, *A Defence of Virginia (and Through Her the South) in Recent and Pending Contexts Against the Sectional Party*. It was written by Robert Lewis Dabney (1820-1898), American Christian theologian, Southern Presbyterian pastor, and Confederate army chaplain. This primary source text was selected because it is considered representative of the Southern Conservative culture of the 19th century. An online book review at puritanboard.com claims that "By understanding Dabney's mind, we have a window in which to see the minds of an entire sociological group"

Dabney (1867) begins his treatise by introducing his reader to the seriousness of his topic. He attacks the "perverted judgment of the antislavery party" and deems its supporters "beyond the reach of reasoning" (p. 5) while pointing out the grave threat they pose to "just government and Christian order" (p. 6). He presents himself and those who think like him as stable and independent, rational minded and righteous, holding on to their convictions - unlike the thoughtless "victims" who had been fooled and led astray by the arbitrary and unfounded ideas of the abolition movement. He encourages his reader to not lose hope for the future, no matter what the current circumstances, claiming that one day the slavery issue will be dead, "its mischievous principles…completely a thing of the past" (p. 6). It can be seen as ironic that his prayers were answered – the mischievous principles of the slavery issue are indeed a thing of the past in current day America - however, not in the way that Dabney intended, for he wished that the voices of the abolitionists would fade like an insignificant blot in history without effecting the existing social order of the society in which he lived. "To the rational historian who, two hundred years hence, shall study the history of the nineteenth century, it will appear one of the most curious vagaries of human opinion, that the Christian and philanthropy of our day should have given so disproportionate an attention to the evils of African slavery" (p. 9).

Counter arguments against Abolitionists

Dabney continues his defense by counter-arguing some of the attacks of the abolitionists on slavery. For example, abolitionists condemn slavery partly because of the brutality it often produces in one human being (the slaveholder) towards another (the slave). Dabney than argues that brutality is not being sanctioned. Moreover, it says nothing about the institution of slavery itself. "For, unfortunately, the human race is a fallen race – depraved, selfish, unrighteous and oppressive, under all institutions" (p. 24). He shifts the accusations of evil from the institution of slavery towards mankind as whole. Thus making the institution of slavery a clear example of, rather than a contradiction to, the Christian paradigm – for the Christian paradigm taught him that all man are born sinners. Mary Douglas might see this as an example of one of the five ways of dealing with anomalies (see the 'theory' chapter of this thesis) – namely, *redefining* it so that it will start to make sense within a particular paradigm. Dabney *redefined* slavery as a symptom of, rather than a cause for, cruelty in human beings.

Whereas abolitionists may argue that slavery dehumanizes and commodifies people by making them the property of someone else, Dabney retorts that, "it is not the person, but the labour of the slave, which is the master's property" (p. 94). This arguments separates the 'slave' (person) from 'slavery' (his labor), and tries to make a distinction between who one *is* - in one's essence - and what one *does*, is forced to do, or is restricted from doing. Taking this point of view, Dabney can say that slavery does not dehumanize, because a master will never have property over the slave's soul –and the soul, according to his Christian paradigm, is the unique part that makes us human and makes one human different from another. Nothing, not even slavery, could jeopardize that.

Religious Justifications

Dabney provides further religious arguments to rationally place slavery within the 'intended' order of human society and thereby justify the institution. He refers to a biblical story found in Genesis chapter 9: Noah's youngest son, Ham, sees his father naked and tells his brothers, who then walk backwards into their sleeping father's tent, so as not to look at him, and cover his naked body with a blanket. When Noah wakes up and finds out what happened, he proclaims a curse upon Canaan, the son of Ham. "A curse on Canaan! He will be a slave to his brothers" (Genesis 9: 25).

In Dabney's time there was a widespread belief that Africans where the descendents of Canaan, the son of Ham. Dabney (1867) adds: "These descendants were included in the punishment of their wicked progenitors on that well-known principle of God's providence, which 'visits the sin of the fathers upon the children'... so that not only punishment, but the sinfulness, becomes hereditary" (p. 102). Africans thus became defined as a different kind of people. Slavery, and the different positions accorded to white vs. black people within this system (white = master; black = slave), had become not only institutionalized but also reified in the minds of Southern slave-owners. Another example of reification is found in the words of Confederate vice-president, Stephens who, "rejected the doctrine of racial equality and declared that the confederacy was 'founded on exactly the opposite idea; its foundations are laid, its cornerstone rests, upon the great *truth* that the negro is not equal to the white man; that slavery, subordination to the superior race, is his *natural* and *normal* condition. This, our new government, is the first, in the history of the world, based on this great physical, philosophical, and moral truth" (Stephens, March 30, 1861, quoted fin Howard, 1999, p. 35, emphasis/italicization mine).

Slavery was seen as God's assigned place for Africans. Slave-owners could thus argue that the institutionalization of slavery was not a sin – as the abolitionists would claim – but a consequence of sin. It was put in place by God, as a "safeguard against the depraved [descendants of Ham]" (Dabney, p. 103). Dabney argues that, so long as Africans complied with their position as slaves within the order of God's creation, they could still be acceptable to God despite the sin of their forefather. Conversely, it was believed that, "without being so [slaves], they can neither be the faithful servants of God, nor be held as regular members of the Christian Church" (Furman, 1838, p. 8).

To back up this argument, Dabney points to New Testament rules which set the guidelines of proper conduct for slaves. For example: "Slaves, obey your earthly masters with respect and fear, and with sincerity of heart, just as you would obey Christ" (Ephesians 6:5, NIV), "Slaves, obey your earthly masters in everything; and do it, not only when their eye is on you and to win their favor, but with sincerity of heart and reverence for the Lord" (Colossians 3:22, NIV), "Slaves, submit yourselves to your masters with all respect, not only to those who are good and considerate, but also to those who are harsh" (1 Peter 2:18). Dabney also points out the rules that were set in place for masters of slaves, for example: "Teach slaves to be subjected to their masters in everything, to try to please them, not to talk back to them" (Titus 2:9), "Masters, provide your slaves with what is right and fair, because you know that you also have a Master in heaven" (Colossians 4:1, NIV). In accordance with his view on slavery, Dabney interprets these verses as having been written down so that the institution could function as "suitable to the character of the depraved persons for whom it was designed, and wholesome and benign. Hence [God and Moses] prohibit all inhuman abuses of it; and then they do not tolerate it merely as an unavoidable wrong; but they expressly legalize it, as right" (p. 118).

Slavery was thus seen as a merciful institution – giving the descendents of Ham a second chance to be accepted by God, under certain conditions. "[Slavery] was appointed by God as the punishment of, and remedy for (nearly all God's providential chastisements are also remedial) the peculiar moral degradation of a part of the [human] race" (Dabney, p. 103). This argument entails that if white people stopped enslaving Africans, or if Africans refused to be slaves – refused to conform to their identity and role as slaves as established by God through the institution of slavery – the souls of these poor Africans would be in mortal danger, because of the curse that was brought upon them by their forefather, Ham.

Essentially, then, what the institution of slavery did was create a clear dividing line between white people and black people. They could both be Christians but different criteria applied for them to be accepted as Christians – not only within the social order but also presumably by God, as he was presumed to be the founder of that social order. "It is enough for us to say (what is capable of overwhelming demonstration) that for the African race, such as Providence has made it, and where He has placed it in America, slavery was the righteous, the best, yea, the only tolerable relation" (p. 25). Africans had to conform to their role as slaves in order to be saved, which, in turn, meant that white people, as the superior race, were responsibly for enslaving them and propagating the institution. Hence the strong moral sentiments against the abolition of slavery.

Anti-Abolitionist Discourse

Dabney uses the discourse of **purity vs. danger** – e.g. "…that in the slaveholding South was…the greatest social stability and purity" (p. 12), "But in the Church, abolitionism lives, and is more rampant and mischievous than ever, as infidelity; for this is its true nature…abolitionism still lives in its full activity…a fell spirit which is the destroyer of every hope" (p. 6), "…the South is now subjected…[to] the degrading and debauching of the moral sensibility and principles of the helpless victim" (p. 7), "we rely on the force of truth to explode all dangerous error" (p. 22) etc. – **honest vs. impure motives** – e.g. "it did not suit their selfish purposes, that Europeans should know, that in this slaveholding South was the true conservative power of the American Government, the most solid type of old English character…and above all, the very fountain of international commerce and wealth; lest Europe should desire to visit and to trade with this section itself. And the readiest way to prevent this, was to paint the South to all the rest of the world, in the bleakest colours of misrepresentation" (p. 12), - **rationality vs. foolishness** – "the principles…are simply those of common sense… they shall commend themselves to every honest mind" (p. 27), "…had persuaded themselves; but were, in fact, conceited, overweening, and fantastic" (p. 9), etc. - **eternal truth vs. false whim** - e.g. "…after the tumult of faction shall have spent its rage, upon the foundations of truth and justice" (p. 8), "there is a higher law" (p. 17), "make our cause practically the cause of truth and order" (p. 22), etc. - **order vs. disorder** – e.g. "…save America from chronic anarchy and barbarism" (p. 8), etc. - **honor vs. degradation**– "men at the South who have not been unmanned and debauched…these are the men whom Providence will call forth from their seclusion" (p, 8), "treating us as if our guilt was too clear to admit any argument, or we were too inferior to be capable of it" (p. 14), "we must be respected: and to defend our good name" (p. 20), etc.

In all of the above-mentioned arguments and various discourses that can be found in his text, Dabney (1867) is representative not only of the anti-abolitionist Southern slaveholder, but, in the more general sense, of a human being who feels threatened by changes in the existing social order which shake and put into question his established view on reality. This idea will be explored further in the chapter about homosexuality and the church.

The end of slavery

Blackburn (1988) argues that the end of slavery had much less to do with economic circumstances than may be rationally suspected. A rationalistic approach would assume that the system of slavery would die out, or could be abolished, as its economic advantages declined. However, despite significant economic consequences, "slave emancipation was put on the agenda by englobing political crises and social contestation" (Blackburn, p. 521).

Furthermore, Blackburn (1988) has shown that the abolition of slavery was not an isolated change in American society at the time but could only be achieved in the context of greater encompassing social changes. While anti-slavery sentiments may have been present in individual minds, these did not lead to institutional change as long as the greater institution of society remained stable. A certain amount of tension was required to activate social movements and bring about the abolition of slavery. Moreover, the success of abolitionists relied not on appeals to slaveholders' conscience, but on the changes and enforcement of new laws (Blackburn 1988). Stubborn slaveholders could not simply be persuaded with words. The way society was organized and structured had to change first, and individual conscience would follow later. These observations are in line with social psychological research.

Attitude Change

Social Psychologists (Aronson, Wilson, & Akert, 2007) discovered the power of internal justifications or self-persuasion – which can be brought about by leading someone to act a certain way without much external pressure or persuasion. In one experiment, for example, children were each shown a number of toys in a room and asked to rate their attractiveness. The experimenter than pointed to the toy that had been rated most attractive by the child and told the child that he or she was not allowed to play with that particular toy. Half the children were given a threat of severe punishment if they played with the toy, the other half was threatened with a mild punishment. While the experimenter left the room, giving the children time to play with the other toys, none of the children played with the forbidden toy. Later, the experimenter returned to the room and again asked the children to rate each of the toys' attractiveness. The forbidden toy was still rated as highly desirable, or even more desirable than it initially had been, by the children who had received a threat of severe punishment; its attractiveness had dropped significantly for those children who had received only a threat of mild punishment and still refrained from playing with the toy. The lasting effects of this attitude change were further validated in a replicated experiment by Freedman (1965) who extended by initial experiment: Several weeks later, the children were individually invited back to the experimenters room, which still contained the same toys as last time, supposedly to take a paper-and-pencil test, under the guidance of a different experimenter than the one that had told them they were not allowed to play with one of the toys. After the child finished his or her test, the new experimenter would announced that she was going to leave the room to grade the test, which would take a while, and that the child could play with any of the toys he or she liked. Aronson et al. (2007) conclude that while the great majority of the children who had previously received a severe threat now happily played with the initially forbidden toy, "The overwhelming majority of the children whom Freedman had mildly threatened several weeks earlier decided, on their own, not to play with [it]" (p. 177). Aronson et al. (2007) explain that, seeking an internal justification for not playing with the toy even though they had wanted to initially, the children had successfully convinced themselves they didn't really like the toy anyway. It had lost its appeal.

Changing attitudes towards slavery

In a similar way, changing an institution – e.g. changing the laws so that people can no longer own slaves - may eventually effect individually, as well as socially, held attitudes towards that institution. For instance, now-a-days, there are very few people in the Southern states of America who still hold the same views as Dabney (1867) and believe that slavery is right. But this change in the general attitude did not come about until well after the actual abolition of slavery. The Emancipation Proclamation gave legitimacy to a new social order – supported by the abolitionists - and a new social reality was within reach. Lincoln altered society in ways that would have been unimaginable – and therefore, perhaps, frightening to some – at his time. Not everyone was happy about these significant changes. It cost Abraham Lincoln his life. He was assassinated. By introducing the Emancipation Proclamation, Lincoln changed not only the law concerning slavery, but with it altered the structure of society, which eventually led to a shift in attitudes of its members.

As Douglas (1986) has argued, institutions influence individual cognition. It can be said that the mind or consciousness of an individual adapts to the structure of his or her society, as a way of legitimizing its reality and feeling secure within it. The mind provides justifications and explanations for the way things are socially organized. Actions give rise to believes, though it may appear to be the other way around. For instance, Southern slaveholders may have claimed, 'We believe Africans to be the descendents of Ham – whom God has cursed – and that is why they are our slaves.' Whereas the facts of history can be construed to show that, after European Christians began enslaving Africans, they needed a justification to reduce the cognitive dissonance brought about by this action and hence the theology of Ham was constructed and believed. People are capable of creating classifications, order, and meaning - justifying and explaining their own actions along with the collectively constructed social reality. The following sections will explore this idea further.

Race as a socially constructed category and marker of identity

Opinions differ on the causal relation between slavery and racism in America. Was slavery the outcome of an already existing European negative prejudice towards the black 'other,' or did this attitude develop as a result of the institutionalization of slavery in the Americas?[1] From what can be inferred by studying pre-slavery art, laws, personal correspondences, and other primary source documents, this paper will argue for the later case. The changing expressions in art, law, and other historical documents show that black people became differently constituted from, and by, white people. Once made, this distinction was collectively maintained through the 'othering' of black people in art and through discriminatory laws.

Art

The slave trade had a greatly significant effect on Europeans' perception of Africans as 'the other.' This effect can best be noted when one observes representations of African people by 15th and 16th century European artists and compares these to similar representations created later, when the slave trade was well established and ever since. One notices that the dark skin color - still commonly used to classify African people in comparison to Europeans - was not a salient feature in early Europeans' depictions of Africans, as these examples from the 16th century show:

---

[1] Noel's (1972) reader *The Origins of American Slavery and Racism* presents a good overview of articles from both sides of the debate.

Theodore de Bry
African Slaves Working in a Sugarmill, engraving. 1596

Reproduced in *Grand Voyages* (1590-1634): part V (1594).
Courtesy of the Royal Library, The Hague. (Brienen, 2006, p. 137)

Albert Durer
Portrait of Katherine 1521

('Black is Beautiful' 2008)

Woman of the Congo

1596
Reproduced in:
Philippo Pigafetta,
*De beschryvinghe vant groot ende
vermaert coninckrijk van Congo*
(Italian edition 1591).

Notice that the 'woman of the Congo' and the 'African Slaves...' are not depicted as very different from European people in their physical appearance. The' portrait of Katherine' is more detailed and shows the distinct facial features of Africans, but a dark complexion is not a prominent feature of this portrait. When one looks at these pictures, one realizes that this is not how Africans would be artistically portrayed by white people now-a-days. Somewhere along the process of justifying their increasingly more barbaric treatment of Africans, Europeans evidently found need to delineate the differences between themselves and the African 'other' more clearly. The slave trade thus created a new classification, a new salient marker of identity - ones race, as defined by ones skin color. This has remained a, to us, very prominent characteristic of classification.

Laws and other written documents

As mentioned before, white plantation owners initially regarded their black slaves in much the same way as they did their white servants. Moreover, there is evidence that white servants on the plantation regard black slaves as their equals. Morgan (1975) recounts that they often sided with each other and mingled with each other without reserve, despite the different skin colors. This fact may not seem surprising, given their shared subordinate condition. However, sharing a similar socioeconomic status does not automatically lead to acceptance between racial groups. Modern-day attitudes of America's lower class white population towards African Americans - which are significantly racist - is a case in point (Morgan p. 327). Furthermore, checking historical documents Handlin (1972) observes that before the 1660s there was no word to describe children of racially mixed parents (later referred to as "mulattos"), demonstrating the lack of racial classifications (p. 33).

Religion was the salient feature of identity – the primary marker between "us" and "them" in American society at the time. "The priority of religious over color prejudice is amply demonstrated by analysis of the early laws and court decisions pertaining to Negro-white sexual relations. These sources explicitly reveal greater concern with Christian-non-Christian than with white-Negro unions" (Noel, 1972c, p. 117). Over time, the chief concern with religion became more and more implicit and the lines of distinction gradually shifted towards a greater concern about race over religion.

The first step is indicated by laws of the 1660s that regulate interracial marriages, However Noel (1972c) notes that although these laws had started using racial terminology on the surface, on a deeper level they were still referring to and emphasizing underlying religious, national, or other non-racial distinctions. For example, a Maryland law of 1681 described marriages of white women with Negroes as lascivious and "to the disgrace not only of the English butt also [sic] of many *other Christian* Nations" (117). Morgan (1975) also suggests that these laws "could reflect religious rather than racial feeling: that a Christian should not lie with a heathen" (p. 333). Thus, while sources show that a distinction was beginning to be made between white and black people, skin color itself was not yet the most important marker of classification. Rather, black skin was being equated with 'heathen,' which marked the significant difference between Africans and Europeans.

African slaves were definitely seen as a distinct social category from white Americans by the 18th century, and the distinction was wholly based on skin color. Recall that enslaved Africans in the Americas lacked a sense of shared identity, and Douglas' (1986) observation that as new classifications are being constructed, people step forward to accept and identify themselves with these labels. A notably example of this idea is the account of former slave, Tabo Janszoon, who changed his own name to Adriaan *de Bruin* (meaning, *the Brown*) sometime after he was set free with an inheritance after the death of his kind master, Adriaan van Bredehoff, in 1733 ('Black is Beautiful' 2008). Adriaan de Bruin clearly self-identified himself as a brown person. It is conceivable that he might not have used this marker of identity, or put himself in this category, under different circumstances. Had the institution been different, Adriaan de Bruin might never have thought to classify himself based on skin color. Such a category might not even have existed.

Full slave codes appear in the law after 1700 (Handlin, 1972, p. 34). Black people were governed by separate laws from those that applied to white people. Interesting are the laws that describe the prohibition of interracial marriages and sexual relationships. These laws can be viewed the same way as the Levitican rules of avoidance of impure animals analyzed by Douglas (1999), which were reviewed in the *classifications confer identity* section of the theoretical part of this thesis. Just as the rules of the Leviticans were neither arbitrary nor universal but part of a specific system of classification, so these 'laws of avoidance' of interracial relationships were in no way arbitrary. They were a structural part of the society. The whole institution depended on keeping the distinction between black and white intact – so much had been build around this myth. Interracial marriages would produce anomalous children – neither black nor white. A population of such anomalous would de-legitimatize the whole system and throw the social world into chaos and confusion. From this perspective, one can also better understand the social psychological and cultural bases of Dabney's (1867) line of reasoning and the vigor with which he defended slavery. It was not solely about an institution, but about a constructed reality that needed to be maintained.

Paradigm shifts – changing views towards race and slavery.

The previous section noted that markers of classification in America gradual shifted from religious to racial differences. How did the dividing line between superiority and inferiority shift from Christian vs. heathen to white skin vs. black skin? It may have stemmed from the dilemma of what to do with slaves that had accepted the Christian faith. Initially, in the colonies, such former slaves were free by law (D'Anjou, 1996; Morgan, 1975). The belief prevailed that, as Christians, they should be seen as equals. Morgan (1975) explains that, "before the 1660s it seems to have been assumed that Christianity and slavery were incompatible" (p. 331). How could one justify keeping a brother or sister in Christ under oppression? But if an increasing number of African slaves embraced the Christian faith, and each one was then freed, who would work on the plantation? As this paper has presented so far – see the discussion on Dabney's (1867) text as an example -Conservative Christians of America did collectively develop a way to cope with this dilemma and came to justify the system of slavery, unflinchingly, even from a religious perspective. White and black people could both be Christians, but in order to truly qualify as a Christian, blacks would have to be slaves – subordinate and obedient to their masters of the superior race, as constituted by God and recorded in the Bible – they argued.

How did it come to this? Why did European Christians move from regarding all Christians as equal, to making such a fundamental distinction between white and black Christians? The following section will explore these questions further.

Why and how did attitudes towards people with black skin change?

Nash (1972) explains that, "it was hardly possible for one people to enslave another without developing strong feelings against them" (p. 146). Social Psychologists (Aronson, et al.

2007) refer to this effect as "blaming the victim" (p. 401). It is produced by the cognitive dissonance of wanting to see oneself as a 'good' person, but at the same time observing ones ability and apparent willingness hurt another human being. It explains why victims of rape are often portrayed as having been promiscuous or 'asking for it,' by their perpetrator, and why 'the enemy' in war is dehumanized. It is also another example of the, by now, well-known (social) psychological finding that attitudes are often derived from actions and the need to justify these actions. So, if there was an initial bias towards black people, it was confirmed and strengthened by the act of keeping them as slaves. "Racism arose, in response to slavery, as a means of justifying the extreme economic exploitation of blacks" (Noel, 1972b, p. 153). Examples of racist stereotyping can be observed in Dabney's (1867) text: "[it is] asserted that there is still much degrading ignorance among Southern negroes" (p. 215), "The Africans...were the most debased among pagan savages" (p. 216), "The slave was not permitted to testify against a white man, and this was a restriction made proper by his low grade of truthfulness, his difference of race..." (p. 220). Apparently there was an underlying conflict between people's conscience and their deeds, which gave rise to racial stereotypes and beliefs of black inferiority.

Peabody & Grinberg (2007) and Noel (1972b) paradoxically mark the emerging abolitionist movement as the catalyst towards such racist attitudes. The voices of abolitionists revealed the discrepancy between the European egalitarian value system and the system of slavery (Noel, 1972b), arousing cognitive dissonance and the psychological need to justify. Noel (1972) claims that this egalitarian value system had its roots in the Judaeo-Christian heritage and was later taken over by Enlightenment philosophy, which abandoned the authority of the Church (Tignor et al. 2008). Noel (1972) argues that exploitation and ethnic stratification alone are insufficient causes to account for the rise of racism: "Exploitation and slavery have existed without racism" (p. 164). It was in the context of a certain value system - which necessitated the construction of a rationale with which to incorporate an otherwise contradictory institution within this moral system - that racism developed. Dabney's (1867) text can be read and analyzed as supportive of this claim. Racism became the rational justification that allowed slavery to continue in a society based on freedom and equality for all men, by making a distinction between white (superior) and black (inferior) men. Noel (1972b) notes that, "Eventually, racism became an autonomous value complex with a significance of its own apart from the institution which generated it" (p. 163). In other words, racism became reified.

Observing social change

The changing views on race went hand-in-hand with an increasing degree of conviction about the morality of slavery. The two seem to have nourished each other. When reading the fiery arguments of Christian anti-abolitionist in defense of slavery, it seems almost unimaginable that, "When the English first thought about colonizing America, they planned to liberate Indians and blacks enslaved by the Spanish and to rehabilitate their unemployed countrymen in an integrated New World community" (Morgan, 1975, front cover). Moreover, at one point in history, it was primarily the Christians who opposed slavery – while secular, Enlightenment thinkers argued against them. For example, Andrew Fletcher, a "Scottish prophet of the Enlightenment …attacked the Christian church not only for having promoted the abolition of slavery in ancient times but also for having perpetuated the idleness of the freedmen thus turned loose on society. The Church by setting up hospitals and almshouses had enabled men through the succeeding centuries to life without work" (Morgan, 1975, p. 325). Stark (2004) explains that slavery became institutionalized in the New World under "strenuous papal opposition" (p. 291).

When looking back on history – trying to plot out who argued what (e.g. the church – for or against slavery) and when – it becomes evident that the views of social groups change, and sometimes completely turn around. Boskin (1972) quotes Daniel Bell (*The End of Ideology*. New York: The Free Press, 1961, 440. n. 169) in saying, "…the history of moral temper is, I feel, one of the most important ways of understanding social change, and particularly the irrational forces at work in men" (Boskin, p. 104). Moral views are not fixed or an essential part of a group identity - an identity is itself socially constructed and not something essential. This makes 'social groups' hard to define. For instance, both the abolitionist and staunchly conservative Southern slave-owners tended to define themselves as Christians. Religious arguments were used on both sides of the slavery debate.

> Certain writers on politics, morals and religion…have advanced positions…very
> unfriendly to the principle and practice of holding slaves; and by some these sentiments
> have been advanced among us, tending in their nature… indirectly to deprive the slaves
> of religious privileges, by awakening in the minds of their masters a fear that
> acquaintance with the Scriptures… would naturally produce the aforementioned effects;
> because the sentiment in opposition to the holding of slaves have been attributed, by their
> advocates, to the Holy Scriptures, and to the genius of Christianity. These sentiments, the

Convention, on whose behalf I address your Excellency, cannot think just, or well-founded: For the right of holding slaves is clearly established by the Holy Scripture... (Furman, 1838, p. 4).

And yet - despite the fact that both the social groups and the opinions they hold so dear are socially constructed and adaptable – opposition between social groups seems constant throughout history. As one group moves to change its position, so does the other, so that the distance between them remains unchanged.

Conclusion and Commentary

Institutionalization

Although it had been abandoned in European society after the rise of Christianity, slavery became reinstituted in the New World, due to the materialistic aspirations of, and competition between, developing European nations inspired by colonialism. The institutionalization of slavery was not a political decision made without any moral reserve. Rather, it was a gradual processes relying on a combination of economic circumstances and myths and ideologies to legitimize it.

These ideologies stemmed from the English' concern with poverty and the moral value of work. They developed systems of enforced labor in cities such as London, which offered a successful social solution to the poverty issue in their eyes. The value of one's life began to be associated with hard work and a 'civilized' life style. With increasing migration and contact with 'others,' this new ethic did not remain contained within England but began to be imposed on American Indian natives and later on Africans transported to the Americas. Europeans thus assumed they were increasing the value of the 'savage's' life by imposing hard work and European 'civilized' culture on him.

African slaves were at first treated and perceived very much like European servants. However, the European poor were eventually able to escape their lot as exploited laborers in American society, while the fate of the Africans steadily declined as they became a permanently enslaved social class. It wasn't that Europeans were reluctant to enslave members of their own race and therefore chose the Africans to be their slaves. Rather, Africans in the Americas were especially vulnerable to exploitation and enslavement mainly because they had not developed a social identity and therefore lacked group solidarity and agency in American society.

Restructuring

Slavery became embedded in, and a structural part of, American society. There may have been people who disagreed with the morality of the system, but there was little they could, or attempted to, do. To reject slavery would have meant to reject an entire social order which seems an 'impossible thought' (referring to Merton; see Douglas, 1986). For example, in current society, there may be people who have strong feelings against the school system, but what can they do? The institution of education is part of our social reality. If one refuses to comply and does not get an education, one will have great difficulty finding a job, and without a job one cannot expect to earn money, and without money one cannot survive in this world – in the society we have constructed. Protest was not sufficient to bring about the changes in the social order required to make possible the abolition of slavery. Tension and social restructuring was needed, and it came with war.

Under the leadership of Abraham Lincoln, as a result of civil war, a new union was constructed. There was no place for slavery in this new union, though it had seemed an indispensable part in the old order. This is an example of two different paradigms – one that supported and one that abhors slavery – that existed side by side in America and fought for power and legitimacy until the later replaced the former. The whole institution of society had to be reordered and restructured – in fact, the era after the civil war is commonly referred to as the Reconstruction Era – so that a new paradigm could be constructed and slavery abolished. "The moment came when I felt that slavery must die that the nation might live!" (President A. Lincoln, 1864. Quoted in Howard, 1999, p. 187). The creation of the new union went hand in hand with, and allowed, the abolition of slavery. *Liberty and Union, now and forever, one and inseparable.* (Webster, 1830. Quoted in Howard, p. 190).

The fact that the institution of slavery had become reified in the minds of individuals can be observed in Dabney's (1867) text that expresses the view held by many conservative Christians at the time that God had bound Africans, as the descendents of Ham, to a life of slavery. Dabney explains that: "These descendants were included in the punishment of their wicked progenitors on that *well-known principle* of God's providence, which 'visits the sin of the fathers upon the children'… so that not only punishment, but the sinfulness, becomes hereditary" (p. 102, emphasis mine). However, it is interesting to note that this theology – this "well-know principle" - has been abandoned. In the current age, very few Christians still hold to the belief that a person's 'punishment' will be carried on to the next generation. Many would quote the words of Jesus that "neither this man nor his parents sinned [that he was born blind]" (John 9:3). For further research it might be interesting to find out when exactly this theology – that 'the sins of the fathers' are passed on to the children – began to circulate and when it was abandoned, and then to see if any correlation can be made with the institutionalization and the abolition of slavery.

Slave owners produced fiery arguments against the abolitionists and the abolition movement. Their tenacity in defending the slavery system and steadfast belief in its moral-rightness provides clues that the successful abolitions of slavery would not come about through appeals to slaveholders' conscience. As social psychological research shows that attitudes are derived from actions and the minds ability to justify and make sense of these actions, changing people's attitudes can best be brought about by manipulating their actions to make their attitudes align with the new way of doing things. The Emancipation Proclamation freed the African slaves, thus creating the possibility for white people to stop seeing black people as slaves by definition, thereby starting the process of changing commonly held attitudes towards slavery. Individual attitudes adapt to the structure of the collective social system. Redefining the system, the Union of the states of America, created a new cognitive map for the people on which to base their values and believes.

New Reality

Although slavery became abolished, the system had left a permanent mark on the social reality of American society. Slavery, as this paper has argued, introduced a new, divisive, marker of classification between people. Race, based on skin color, become the way to distinguish between 'us' and 'them.' Slavery not only produced the social distinction between black and white people, but also led to racist stereotyping and believes of white supremacy. These developments can be explained by the social psychology theories of 'cognitive dissonance' and 'blaming the victim.' The racial stereotypes and inequalities that proceeded the social construction of race itself proved even more difficult to erase than the institution – namely, slavery – from which they can all be said to have derived.

Chapter 3 - Gay Liberation

In the previous chapter we saw how Africans were turned into slaves in the Americas. It was argued that the concept of race, and especially the subordination of black people based on their skin color, was constructed together with the institution of slavery and shaped by it. Eventually, the institution of slavery was abolished but the effects it had had on race lingered on and can still be felt today. We now move on to a contemporary case of discrimination against a particular group of people: namely, homosexuals in American society. As this chapter will show, the two issues are comparable and this comparison can be useful in furthering the gay liberation movement. However, while the abolition of slavery occurred centuries ago, the gay liberation movement is comparatively young and not fully realized in the U.S. This is where the main differences between the two issues lies, making the evolution of the social rejection vs. acceptance of homosexual people more difficult to document but potentially also more valuable and significant in today's world.

Many sources could be found about the institutionalization, the effects on society and race, and the abolition of slavery. It was possible to piece together a coherent story and come up with a conclusive picture. However, when the same was attempted for the issue of discrimination against homosexual people, it proved to be much more difficult. Possibly because it is such a contemporary issue, and the gay liberation movement is still a work-in-progress in the United States, I had difficulty finding secure analytical and reflective discussions on this issue. Scholars have had plenty of time to come up with strong theories concerning the institutionalization of slavery in the Americas. Likewise, the abolition movement is well documented. But just like the gay liberation movement itself, the story of how the discrimination against homosexual people developed is in no way complete.

I will compare the discourse of discrimination used by anti-abolitionist and anti gay-rights Christians. Then I will offer some theories concerning the construction of homosexuality and the development of negative attitudes towards homosexual people - most of these theories center on modernization and the changing perceptions of gender roles, which also may have changed sexual norms. However, I must add that these theories are rather one-sided and in no way conclusive. Like I said earlier, I believe this limitation – in comparison to the previous chapter's study on slavery and the abolition movement - can be attributed to the fact that the discussion and research on homosexuality is only just getting started. In time - and with further scholarly research, discussions, and debates – more solid arguments concerning the institutionalization, effects, and ending of discrimination against homosexuals may emerge.

Then and Now

Christians who are advocating gay rights often point to the abolition of slavery and the changing views of the church towards slavery, as discussed in the previous chapter, as an argument for the plausibility of social change and revision of church doctrine. Presbyterian pastor Rogers (2006), for example, draws the comparison between how the Bible was interpreted in the 19th century to justify slavery and how it is being interpreted today to condemn homosexuality as one of his main argument for recommending the Presbyterian church to widen its acceptance towards homosexual people. Johnson (2007), professor of New Testament at Chandler School of Theology, Emory University uses the same argument to reassure Christians that the acceptance of homosexuals as full members of society and the church community will not pose a threat to having faith in the Bible or the legitimacy of the church.

In fact - just as Christian abolitionist (e.g. Wesley, 1774) began to proclaim that the abolition of slavery was in the best interest of the church - both Rogers (2006) and Johnson (2007) argue that the continuing discrimination towards homosexual people poses a far greater threat than their acceptance would pose to the Christian church. Archbishop Emeritus Desmond Tutu expresses the same opinion: "It is not acceptable for us to discriminate against our brothers and sisters on the basis of sexual orientation just as it was not acceptable for discrimination to exist on the basis of skin colour under Apartheid... the very future of Anglicanism depends upon [a deeper and more open conversation about the issue of homosexuality] taking place" (Dormor and Morris 2007, p. ix). These are just a few examples of current church leaders who are dedicated to bringing about change, writing compelling texts to help conservative Christians open up their minds and reconsider their stance on homosexuality.

On the internet, too, there is a web of activity going on to change the situation for homosexual people in America and end discrimination, especially the discrimination coming from the church. ReligiousTolerance.org includes an essay on religious change - which discusses the churches changing views towards slavery as well as the current debate on homosexuality – to highlight the occurrence and necessity of revisions in Christian teachings and attitudes towards societal issues. ReligiousTolerance.org "consider[s] this the most important section of [their] website" (Ontario Consultants on Religious Tolerance 2006, p. 1). Furthermore, there are support groups on the web for gay Christians (Gay Christian Network; Evangelicals Concerned; Beyond ExGay). These websites promote the forming of communities and encourage members to support each other, banding together to dispel the conservative church's discrimination against homosexual people.

Of course, this meddling with church doctrine and challenging of long-believed biblical interpretations does not go uncontested. Just as the movement towards the abolition of slavery produced fiery counter-reactions from the conservative Christians of America - as exemplified by the analysis of Dabney's (1867) text in the previous chapter of this thesis - conservative Christians today are bracing against the liberalization of church teachings on homosexuality. Moral entrepreneurs, such as LaBarbera (2009), with internet campaigns like AmericansforTruth.com, warn against the dangers of weakening traditional norms and values for society. And while taking a seemingly sympathetic view towards individuals who 'struggle with their sexual identity' but are trying to 'live their lives in accordance to God's word,' the conservative Christian organization, Focus on the Family, is particularly harsh towards those who seek to create a greater understanding and acceptance of homosexuality within the church. The discourse used by these Christians is similar to that used by anti-abolitionist Christians in the past.

Discourse of Discrimination Chart

Type of Discourse	Anti Abolitionist	Anti Gay-Rights
Purity vs. Danger	"But in the Church, abolitionism lives, and is more rampant and mischievous than ever, as infidelity; for this is its true nature" (Dabney 1867, p. 6).	"Folks…The stabbing murder of WABC reporter George Weber in New York is a terrible tragedy and yet it is instructive about the perils of promiscuous "gay" life. There is simply nothing that approaches the deviance of male homosexuality — especially at its sexual fringes

		— as other victims of gay-on-gay violence over the decades testify from the grave" (LaBarbera, 2009a March 26)
Eternal Truth vs. False Whim	"we rely on the force of truth to exploit all dangerous error" (Dabney 1867, p. 22). "…after the tumult of faction shall have spent its rage, upon the foundations of truth and order" (Dabney p. 8).	"The enemy of God casts doubt on God's clearly articulated order by acknowledging a well-know truth and then supplementing it with a blatant lie. …the truth about the two sexes is exchanged with the lie that male and female are unimportant, interchangeable and even 'fluid' for some individuals" (FOTF 2009, p. 4). "take a stand for truth… against those who would pervert the Gospel of Christ" (LaBarbera, 2009b, March 27).
Honor vs. Degradation	"…men at the South who have not been unmanned and debauched" (Dabney 1867, p. 8). "We must be respected; and to defend our good name" (Dabney p. 20).	"Focus on the Family is dedicated to defending the inherent honor… of the two sexes" (FOTF 2009: 2). "…All of this begs the question: why would anyone expect the American Left …to understand and honor religious liberty and First Amendment freedoms in the United States?" (LaBarbera, 2009c, March 24).

Righteous vs. Ulterior Motives	"On the lawfulness of holding slaves…the Convention think it their duty to exhibit their sentiment…because they consider their duty before God,,. the peace of the State, the satisfaction of scrupulous conscience, and the welfare of the slaves themselves, as intimately connected with a right view of the subject" (Furman, 1838 p. 3). "it did not suit their selfish purposes, that Europeans should know, that in this slaveholding South was the true conservative power of the American Government… lest Europe should desire to visit and to trade with this section itself. And the readiest way to prevent this, was to paint the South to all the rest of the world, in the bleakest colours of misrepresentation" (Dabney, 1867, p. 12).	"It is precisely because we love those who experience same-sex attractions…that we are motivated to intercede in prayer on their behalf and encourage them in the often difficult journey to steward their temptations according to Biblical sexual ethic" (FOTF analyst 2009, p. 1). "Promoting Perversion Pays – Professional Homosexual Activists Draw Massive Salaries" (LaBarbera, 2009d, March 28)
Rationality vs. Foolishness	"The principles [of slavery] are simply those of common sense… they shall commend themselves to every honest mind" (Dabney 1867: p. 27) "[Abolitionists] are not within the reach of reasoning" (Dabney: 5).	"Those with a personal interest in pro-gay and pro-'transgender' theology often twist the scriptures in ways that defy logical and common sense" (FOTF, 2009: p. 3) "The modern gay and 'transgender' movement is systematically

	"[abolitionists'] minds corrupted by sentiments unfriendly to the domestic and civil peace of the community" (Furman, 1838: 8).	working to dismantle the concept of biological sex, which the Bible teach and which the world has heretofore largely understood" (FOTF: 3). "Christian Clarity in the Midst of Confusion" (FOTF: p. 2).
Order vs. Disorder	"The Christian golden rule of doing to others as we would they should do to us, has been urged as an unanswerable argument against holding slaves. But surely this rule is never to be urged against that order of things, which Divine government has established" (Furman, 1838, p. 5)	"Pro-gay and pro-transgender revisionist theology… violates God's clearly articulated and intentional design for the sexes – thereby distorting his image and his plan for sexuality, marriage, family and the just and proper ordering of society" (FOTF 2009, p. 2).

There is some overlap of course. Some of the examples could easily fit into more than one category of discourse. (Which just goes to show, once again, that categories and classifications are never airtight). To compile this chart I used two historical primary sources as examples of 17th Century anti-abolitionist arguments: Rev. Robert Lewis Dabney's (1867) *A Defence of Virginia: (and Through Her, the South) In Recent and Pending Contests Against the Sectional Party*, and Rev. Dr. Richard Furman's (1838) *Exposition of the Views of the Baptists, Relative to the Coloured Population in the United States, in a Communication to the Governor of South Carolina*. For the contemporary arguments against the gay-rights movement I simply went on the internet – specifically to the conservative Christian websites of Focus on the Family and Americans for Truth – and selected the first comparable examples I came across. Many more examples could be found. This chart was constructed to provide a quick overview of the striking similarities in the rhetoric used by Conservative Christians in America today and those of four centuries ago. The causes they argued were different but, as one can see, their ways of arguing are very similar. The next section will provide a more extensive comparison of the two discourses.

Further Similarities between Pro-Slavery and Homophobia

Separating the person from what he does

A very common retaliation of Conservative anti-gay Christians, defending themselves against accusations of hatefulness and discrimination, is that they, "hate the sin, not the sinner." By fabricating a distinction between 'the homosexual' (sinner) and what he does (sin) and claiming to judge only 'the sin' not 'the sinner,' Christians justify for themselves their subordination of a group of people. In this way, they can even come to believe that they truly have 'the sinner's' best interests at heart: "Those trapped in the deception of homosexuality are people in need of healing. They are hurt and broken people who need the touch of the great physician, Jesus Christ. …Pray to have His heart for the homosexual!" (Goeke, 2009).

All this rhetoric seems comparable in its function to Dabney's (1867) argument that "It is not the person, but the labour of the slave, which is his master's property" (p. 94), with which he aimed to devaluating the argument of abolitionists that slavery is wrong as it subordinates and dehumanizes a class of people. Just as conservative Christians are doing today, conservative Christians in the 17th century essentially separated a person's identity from his actions in order to excuse their own treatment of fellow human beings.

Boundaries are there for everyone's protection/good

"We can clearly see God's goodness in setting boundaries – for our own protection – that limit sexual expression to the context of one-man, one-woman marriage and lead to the procreation of new life and the formation of families as the most basic building block of a stable and productive society" (FOTF analyst, 2009, p. 1).

"God as Righteous, All-wise Sovereign, not only… bestows upon them many unmerited blessings and comforts, but subjects them also to privation… with the merciful intention of making all their afflictions, as well as their blessings, work finally for their good; if they embrace his salvation, humble themselves before him, learn righteousness, and submit to his holy will" (Furman 1838, p. 7).

What one can see from these two quotes is the idea that the rules are not arbitrary. They are believed to have been designed by God with clear purpose – namely to procure order and stability in society. Slavery was thought to exist as a "safeguard against the depraved" (Dabney, 1867: 103) – remove the institution and society falls into disarray. Likewise, modern conservative Christians seriously fear disastrous consequences for society if 'God's' rules for human sexuality within the institution of marriage are not upheld.

Double-Standards

It was believed that Africans, as supposed descendents of Ham, were under a curse. Yet while proclaiming this curse upon them, God established the institution of slavery as a way for them to still be saved. 'Evidence' of this was found in Biblical rules of conduct specifically addressed to slaves vs. masters (see, for example, Ephesians 6). Furman's (1838) thus stated that, "Without being [slaves], they can neither be the faithful servants of God, nor be held as regular members of the Christian Church" (p. 8). This argument is very similar to ones used by many of today's conservative Christians saying that openly homosexual people cannot be considered 'good Christians,' nor can they be accepted as active/legitimate members by most conservative churches, unless they suppress their sexuality and do not "act on it." This mode of thinking and its discourse creates distinctions, accompanied by double standards, between Christians: Black Christians must be slaves, according to Conservative (white) Christians of 17th Century America. Gay Christian must be celibate, according to Conservative (heterosexual) Christians of 21st century America.

Another way of analyzing the discourse of discrimination is by taking Douglas' (1976) framework for the possible ways of dealing with anomalies (also see the *Dealing with Anomalies* section in the Reactions part of this thesis).

Dealing with Anomalies

Redefining

Furman (1838) attempts to explain the institution of slavery as an inevitable consequence of sin in the world. Recall that the theology of the time was that God had institutionalized slavery as a measure against the sin of Ham (see *religious justification* section in the Anti Abolitionist Arguments part of this thesis). Furman (1838) seems to say that he has nothing against "seeing [slaves] free" except that he believes society simply wouldn't function that way because of the inherent sinfulness of man. "It is evident, that men are sinful creatures, subject to affliction and to death, as the consequence of their nature's pollution and guilt: That they are now in a state of probation..." (Furman: 7). Dabney (1867) moreover redefined the cruelty produced by the system of slavery as a symptom of the fallen world and the inherent sinfulness of men: "For, unfortunately, the human race is a fallen race – depraved, selfish, unrighteous and oppressive, under all institutions" (p. 24). Slavery did not actually fit the Christian paradigm that all people are equal under Christ and should be treated with love – hence slavery was redefined as a necessary consequence of man's sinfulness while the cruelty it produced was redefined as a clear symptom of men's sinfulness.

Similarly, contemporary Conservative Christians attempt to redefine the occurrence of homosexuality, and intersexuality, in some people as a manifestation of the 'fallen world' in which we live. Homosexuality is seen either as a 'temptation' that Satan plaques certain people with or as a 'brokenness' in people that may have come about either through a traumatic experience, for example, child molestation, or simply through unavoidable contact with the world. Here is a comment from Focus on the Family about intersexuality:

> ...yet, we humans live in a fallen state – and in a fallen world – which impacts us spiritually, emotionally, mentally and even physically. Indeed, there are a number of genetic, biological and congenital conditions that manifest themselves in ways that preclude certain activities and plague our physical existence (Price, 2009, p. 1).

Intersexuality is an umbrella term for various conditions that may cause a person's biological sex to be ambiguous (Hare, 2007). Intersexuality is thus an anomaly that threatens the Christian paradigm that God intended humans as either male or female. It is therefore relabeled in a manner that seems to proliferate another aspect of the Christian paradigm – that sin has entered the world, rendering it imperfect - in order to cover up the contradiction.

Extermination

The practice of exterminating anomalies can furthermore be observed, especially among conservative Christians, towards gay and intersexual people. Homosexuals, especially in

Christian communities in America, are often subjected to change therapies, ministries, and support groups (e.g. Exodus International) in an effort to bring about a change in, or at least successfully repress, their sexual orientation. Extermination can also be clearly observed in the case of intersexuals. Intersexuals are generally assigned a male or female gender. When possible, invasive surgery is used to destroy their unique sex, making it conform to their assigned gender (Bem, 1995; Parker, 2001; Hare, 2007). From the following statement, one can deduce that Focus on the Family favors such surgeries, as well as social coercion, to force intersexuals into an either male or female identity to fit the existing paradigm:

> This condition [intersexuality] can be biological and/or chromosomal in origin and can sometimes be surgically <u>corrected</u>... We – as the Hands and Feet of Christ – are called to help intersexuals carry this "heavy yoke" and steward their assigned gender in a manner that glorifies God and, to the degree possible, reflects His created intent for human sexuality and gender (Price, 2009; emphasis mine).

Rules of Avoidance

Rules of avoidance can be observed most clearly in this exemplary statements, again about intersexuality: "...abundant grace is afforded to those who, for whatever reason, are to bear what Paul refers to as the gift of singleness (1 Cor. 7) ... God readily seeks to strengthen and encourage those who find themselves unable to marry and participate in genderedness and sexual expression as ordained in the created order." (Price, 2009). These statements seem to imply that intersexuals are unable to have sexual intercourse. However - for many intersexuals – "their biological equipment enables them to have sex 'naturally' with both men and women" (Bem, 1995, p. 333). What this statement is implicitly saying, then, is that intersexuals should not express their sexuality. Thus, 'normal' people also should not have sex with an intersexual. Such an activity would violate the "created order." Here, implicit rules for *avoidance* can be observed. Similar rules of avoidance apply to homosexual Christians who are expected to remain celibate if they feel they cannot change their sexual orientation and/or marry someone of the opposite sex.

Labeling as Dangerous

DANGER TO FINANCES — Recent research says that the average person diagnosed with HIV will accumulate $618,000 in additional hospital bills before death. Most homosexuals do not have that much cash on hand, so innocent Americans are paying that either through higher taxes because of payment default or higher health insurance premiums because of this homosexual lifestyle. DANGER TO CULTURE — Homosexual relationships break down the traditional family unit of a father and mother at home which is proven to be the best for raising healthy children. Median age of death for homosexuals is 20 years younger than the general population (Paul Cameron, Ph.D.), leaving children without their parents at a much younger age. And wide-spread homosexual behavior would eventually bring the human species to extinction through lack of procreation. So it would be dangerous to the culture to promote homosexuality. A significant reason that homosexuality is more "dangerous" than terrorism is that our entire country is united against terrorism ... On the other hand, currently much of our society is actually promoting homosexuality — from... favorable treatment of homosexuals in the mass media to the organized attacks on those individuals like State Rep. Sally Kern who simply exercise their First amendment rights to express their opinion against the homosexual agenda (which even results in death threats from this group loudly proclaiming they are not dangerous). The potential danger from terrorism is theoretical and might happen, but the danger from homosexuality is happening — actual, present, and on-going (Jeremiah, 2008).

The long quote above, from the Tulsa Beacon, exemplifies some of the ways in which homosexuals may be thought of as dangerous. The lines of reasoning may seem inconceivable to some, but it is a reality to many conservative Christians in America today.

It can be said that the perceived danger posed by anomalies stems from the threat they pose to classifications. Systems of classification are a part of all societies, and central to religion" (Lambek 2002, p. 194). Anomalies may blur established lines of distinctions and thereby disturb order, a fear that is expressed in the following quote:

An understanding of general and specific distinctions between male and female has remained [throughout time]... Promoting the normalization of homosexuality and 'transgenderism' radically redefines the clearly articulated vision for the sexes outlined in the Bible (FOTF Analyst, 2009, p. 3).

By blurring lines of classification, anomalies or anomalous ideas also undermine the entire system or paradigm that established and relies on those classifications. This underlying fear is explicitly expressed in the following assertion:

The pro-gay revisionist theology threatens to substantially alter the Christian church and biblical doctrine. When God is said to sanction what He plainly forbids, then a serious heresy is unfolding before us in bold fashion" (FOTF Issue Analyst 2008, p. 1).

Moreover, Greenberg (1988) notes that, "Antihomosexual crusades of the past decade have devoted far less effort to recriminalizing sodomy where it has been decriminalized than to block gay-rights bills. Proposition 6 ... barred teachers of any sexual orientation from expressing themselves, in or outside the classroom, in ways that could be construed as favorable to homosexuality" (p. 471). Such a focus indicates that the concern of conservative Christians is not so much with homosexuality per se, or what homosexuals do when they are alone together, but with "shielding [their children] from the knowledge that homosexuality exists and that it is not incompatible with intelligence and respectability" (Greenberg, 471). Since the school and the family unit are the main socializing structures for children in society, it is not surprising that the primary concern of the conservatives is to keep homosexuality out of the school and out of the family by fighting against the homosexual's right to teach in schools (proposition 6), to marry (proposition 8) and/or to adopt children. The underlying fear is for the continuation of the perceived legitimacy of their paradigm. The threat posed by the anomaly is perceived as very real and disconcerting. Homosexuality is therefore labeled as dangerous.

Why?

Since it can be observed that in the discourse of conservative Christians in America homosexuality is treated as an anomaly, I would argue that the discrimination towards homosexual people is based on a particular classification system and its selection criteria that place homosexuals and intersexuals outside its 'natural' categories of sexuality. This classification system, furthermore, can best be understood in the context of the cultures binary paradigm of thinking about gender and human sexuality, which places a strong emphasis on keeping the distinction between male and female, and on the superiority and authority of the male in the family and in society. But where did such a paradigm come from?

The Christian view on sexuality is based on the biblical claim that:

In the beginning the Creator 'made them male and female,' and said, 'for this reason a man will leave his father and mother and be united with his wife, and the two will become one flesh" (Matthew 19:6. NIV).

Many secular people in western society also hold the belief that there are 'naturally' only two sexes and that 'normally' people are attracted to those of the opposite sex. "The secular and the religious are two aspects of the same collective representations" (de Jong, 2007, p. 311). It may be easy then to blame the occurrence of intolerance towards homosexuality in the West solely on the Christian influence and the Bible, but Greenberg (1988) and Boswell (1980) would argue against this simplistic view. The early Christian church broke with many traditions of its Judaic roots – why did it preserve the negative perception of homosexuality? The Bible prohibits many acts, which have received far less attention in Western society than, and have never becoming as stigmatizing as, homosexuality. Furthermore, over the centuries, the church has adjusted many of its doctrines – why is the discrimination against homosexuals only now becoming debatable? In the words of Greenberg (1988), " 'cultural transmission' theory leaves many questions unanswered" (p. 12). Boswell (1980) adds, "At the very most, the effect of Christian Scripture on attitudes toward homosexuality could be described as moot. The most judicious historical perspective might be that it had no effect at all. The source of antigay feelings among Christians must be sought elsewhere" (p. 117). Within Western societies, also among Christians, the level of tolerance towards homosexual behavior has fluctuated. What changes occurred in society and how did they influence social acceptance or rejection of homosexuality?

Modernization and The Impact of Capitalism

In the previous chapter we learned that slavery had once been abandoned in European society, only to be reinstituted after colonization. A turn-around in the general attitude towards, and social acceptance of, slavery could be explained by various contingent factors. But can it be argued that a similar turn-around occurred with regard to the issue of homosexuality? Was homosexuality ever accepted in Western society and by the church? If so, when did it begin to be perceived as a problem? Some scholars (Dormor 2007; Greenberg, 1988; Martin, 2007) theorize that modernity, and specifically capitalism, gave rise to a new way of organizing society in which gender roles became more distinct, and the concepts of marriage and the nuclear family evolved and developed greater significance. Modernity changed the norms for social interaction amongst and between men and women, which in turn had an effect on the way normal and healthy vs. deviant and perilous sexual behavior came to be defined. It is the aim of this chapter to introduce these theories to the reader in order to show that scholarly and academic thought is currently being put into the issue of discrimination against homosexual people. However, the true process of the development of this discrimination still appears vague.

Traditionally, people have pointed out the fact that laws against 'sodomy' were already in place in Western societies long before modernity (Dormor, 2007; Boswell, 1980; Greenberg, 1988; Bullough, 1979) and thus conclude that the social rejection of homosexuality has been rather persistent throughout history. However, some scholars are now asking people to reconsider the definition of words such as 'sodomy' and the extent to which such laws applied to homosexual people in the past. In our society, the term 'sodomy' is often equated with homosexuality. However, Dormor (2007) argues that the term sodomy covered much more than just homosexual acts and that, historically, "tolerance of consensual 'deviant' sexual behavior [may have been] much higher than its status as a capital offense would suggest" (p. 80). Over time, "condemnations of behavior which involved homosexuality only incidentally...came...to be applied to gay people in particular" (Boswell 1980, p. 137). Initially, however, the term, and the laws regarding, 'sodomy' appear to have applied more to, for instance, child molestation and other non-consensual sexual act. Loving and committed relationships between members of the same-sex were probably not understood to involve 'sodomy' (Dormor, 2007) as the next section will suggest.

The Concept of Family and the Place of 'Homosexuals' in Pre-Modern Society

Dormor (2007) asserts that the concept of 'homosexual' as a label of identity did not exist prior to the seventeenth century in Western society. "While there have almost certainly been people exclusively attracted to members of the same sex across all human cultures and throughout history, it is only in the eighteenth century or so that such individuals begin to be defined, by themselves and others, as different" (Dormor, p. 76). How did people, prior to the seventeenth century, with same-sex attractions express their sexuality without being defined by it and set apart from people who did not experience these attractions? Was their behavior tolerated in their society? Dormor (2007) makes the point that the relationship between husband and wife held less romantic significance than it does today and same-sex friendships could be far more intimate. The concept of a nuclear family – consisting of a neat unit of a husband and wife and their children – was probably not as prevalent as it is today. Households were made up of servants, lodgers, business partners, apprentices, etc. These households, as well as society at large, were organized so that members of the same sex spent much of their time together - often sharing one bed. Not surprisingly, "the main bonds of affection" (Dormor, p. 77) generally developed between members of the same-sex. "For two men to share a bed, engage in strong expressions of physical affection like kissing, caressing and hugging, or within certain social strata to write letters expressing their love and affection using language we would expect of lovers, was not only unremarkable, it was central to the fabric of society" (p. 77).

Boswell (1994; see Dormor) even argues that there was a time when the church officially recognized same-sex life-time partnerships. It is unknown to what extent these partnerships resembled our modern idea of 'marriage.' But remember, regular marriages, between a man and woman, in those days did not even resemble our concept of marriage either. What is known is that these "relationships between men, and less often, between women… are described in quasi marital terms and involved profound mutual commitment, sacrifice and affection. Furthermore, such relationships were publicly and ritually formalized in Christian ceremonies" (Bray, 2003; cited in Dormor, 2001). Some of these "committed friends" were even buried together. Although generalizations cannot be made from one example, there is one very clear case of what appears to be a church recognized 'homosexual' marriage as late as the early nineteenth century: Anne Lister and Ann Walker were sworn into a public relationship with each other in a ceremony involving "the exchange of rings and solemnization in church on Easter day in 1834…diaries also account details of their shared sexual intimacy" (Dormor 2007, p. 79).

In other words, the culture of early modern England appears to have provided legitimate space for the expression of what would today be labeled as 'homosexuality.' Such expressions of love were not considered deviant within the structure of that society and may even have been publicly recognized and given consent by the church. [2] But "evolving social structures and ideologies…change sexual socialization and create or close off sexual opportunities" (Greenberg 1988, p. 19). The next part of this thesis will provide thoughts on how modernity destroyed the socially unremarkable and accepted opportunities for homosexual expression of the early modern period. When it was no longer common to share one's bed with a member of the same-sex, and no longer unremarkable for male friends to hug and kiss each other, 'homosexuals' were all of a sudden excluded from what now constitutes 'normal' social life. The walls that included homosexual behavior within the space of accepted social behavior were rearranged and

---

[2] Although it must be added that the later assertion is debatable and contradictory in the face of other sources (Bullough, 1979; Greenberg, 1988) that find evidence in early Christians writings (e.g. Augustine) and state laws that would suggest an overall unfavorable attitude of the church towards homosexuality throughout history.

'homosexuals' were left out and exposed as deviant – as anomalies that did not fit the system. It is in this context that these new 'social-outcasts' began to unite and a new type of identity was constructed, which will be further explored later on in this thesis. But first: How did Western society become organized in such a way as to exclude homosexuals from the 'normal'?

Widening Distinctions and Changing Identities

Greenberg (1988) comments that under feudalism, men and women largely shared the tasks and responsibilities of production and exchange. Husbands and wives formed a "cooperative economic unit" (p. 369) and the division of labor between the sexes was not so noticeable or strict (Sanday, 1981; Greenberg, 1988). It is said that modernity, and the shift to a capitalist society, broke up this unit by separating the 'work' environment from the 'home' environment and taking men away to work while leaving women at home. With men and women being exposed to different environments and expectations their gender identities diverged.

Greenberg (1988) describes that since the start of modernization men have internalized a set of personality traits – for example, rationality, discipline, unemotionality – that came to be known as the bureaucratic or work personality, as the bureaucractic work environment was "until recently… restricted almost entirely to men" (p. 446). The male identity came to be equated with those traits and characteristics that are coincidentally beneficial to men in a capitalist system. Conversely, women were socialized to develop traits suited to their expected role as wives and mothers. Gender roles thus became more distinct. Greenberg (1988) believes that, "The impact of the rise of capitalism broadly transformed the relationship of men and women to production and consumption, thereby changing their relationship to one another" (p. 369).

Male Superiority

Modernity shifted the balance of power between male and female. With the evolution of technology – which promoted the shift to mass production - western societies became increasingly male-oriented (Sanday, 1981). Sanday notes that women lost their position in society as equal contributors in the production process and were "relegated to individual households" (p. 130). Meanwhile, the new mode of production "undermined the collectivity of joint households" (Sanday, p. 130). Sanday (1981) argues that a society becomes oriented towards whichever gender is perceived to be most directly "in touch with the forces upon which people depend for their perceived needs" (p. 11). In a capitalism society, the perceived need is money. Men became the ones that brought in the money. It can be said then that modernity and the spread of capitalism furthered the development of a patriarchal society in which masculinity became affixed with power and esteem whilst femininity was perceived as inferior and crippling.

Beginning in the late 19th century, however, women began to pose a threat to male dominance (Greenberg 1988, p. 387) demanding the right to vote and other social reforms that would encourage more gender equality. The gender roles and male superiority that had been established under the influence of capitalism were beginning to be challenged. "The preservation of male domination in the face of women's aspirations to equality depended on men possessing qualities that clearly differentiated them from women. It consequently became necessary to police men who lacked those qualities just as much as women who exhibited them," Greenberg (1988, p. 387) states. As the distinct gender roles were perceived as important for the functioning of society, they were carefully upheld and perpetuated. For instance, 'feminine' traits – such as nurturance, empathy, and submissiveness - were undesirable to man in a capitalist system and man became concerned with differentiate themselves from the 'feminine' identity so that, "by 1860, 'men no longer dared embrace in public or shed tears'" (Weeks 1981, quoted in Greenberg 1988, p. 388).

According to Greenberg (1988), it was during this time that homosexuality came to be association with femininity in men and lesbianism with masculinity in women – the reversal of gender roles. Greenberg (1988) further notes that lesbianism was possibly not recognized as an existing phenomenon as we know it today, and not included in the homosexual subculture, until the beginning of the twentieth century, "when it became possible for women to live independently of men" (p. 14). The next quote from a contemporary source – the Catholic Education Resource Center - suggests how homosexuality, and especially lesbianism, can still be perceived as a threat to the male identity today. Not only the superiority but also the legitimacy of manhood in current society is thought to be under threat by homosexuality:

...consider the masculine identity. This has already become a major social problem.
Consider the soaring rate at which young men, unlike young women, not only drop
out of school but also commit suicide.[40] We need no fortune-teller to see that
massive social problems, more widespread than the ones we already have, are likely
to emerge whenever and wherever boys or young men are unable to feel deeply
involved in either the family or society as a whole ...Because fatherhood is the one
remaining source of a healthy masculine identity — and we define the latter, once
again, in connection with at least one *distinctive*, necessary, and publicly valued
contribution to society   legalizing gay marriage could leave men with a major

Changing Relationships between Men

Greenberg (1988) provides the argument that capitalism gave rise to increased competition between men which changed gender expectations and the way children, especially boys, were socialized to fit and perpetuate these new definition of manhood vs. womanhood. Parents raise their children according to the norms and values of their society. They hope to install in their children certain traits and characteristics that are expected to be advantages for them in that society. Changing the social context thus changes the way children are socialized - for example, in their gender roles – which further affirms, solidifies, and reproduces the new social order. In order to be a successful man in a capitalist society one needs to develop a level of self-assertiveness and competitiveness. "The competitiveness instilled in boys through parental upbringing, as well as through direct participation in a competitive market economy, would have tended to discourage the acceptance of emotionally intimate relationships between men – whether or not they involved sex" (Greenberg, p. 359). Men became each other's rivals rather than constant companions, as had been the case in the early modern society in England in which men's most important relationships were generally with other man and women's with other women (Dormor, 2007). This change went hand in hand with modernity's changing perception and role of marriage in society.

Marriage and the Family

Modernity saw a shift towards a greater focus on, and social significance of, the nuclear family. One reason for this development was the increasing geographic mobility of people: "In addition to sharpening the sexual division of labor and creating rigidly separated public and private spheres of lives, [modernity produced] greater geographic mobility, which tended to weaken extended kinship ties" (Greenberg 1988, p. 370). Another way in which modernization contributed to the increased focus on the nuclear family was the increased possibility and acceptance of limiting family size. Medical inventions, such as the pill, contributed to the possibility of this and discussions and debates among church leaders eventually led to its acceptance (Martin, 2007).

Not only in society at large but in church doctrine, too, the nuclear family gained greater prominence, whilst the perception and function of marriage altered (Martin, 2007; Greenberg, 1988). Greenberg (1988) notes that 'modern' religion, such as Protestantism, got rid of intermediary actors – such as the priests and saints of the Catholic religion – between people and God. This "required each family to become a miniature church" (Greenberg, p. 371). Whereas historically, the church had had little to do with, or say about the subject, marriage now became sanctified and controlled by the church (Martin, 2007). Martin (2007) notes this shift, observing that marriage used to be seen as an economic arrangement and was performed outside the doors of the church. Then, through various contingencies (see Martin, 2007), it was taken up by the church and the marriage ceremony, symbolically, came to be performed first at the door of, and finally inside the body of, the church. Greenberg (1988) notes that this development occurred not only in the Protestant church but was taken up by the Catholics as well. From the counter-reformation onwards – and not before then - it became a requirement for marriage to be performed by a priest. Rather than being seen as mainly for the practical purpose of reproducing offspring – successors and heirs – in an organized way, marriage now came to be perceived as a means of restraining sexual expression within the 'proper' and God-ordained boundaries. Along with "the procreation of children and the avoidance of fornication" (Martin 2007, p. 69), a third reason for marriage was added to the church wedding service: "The mutual society, help and comfort which the one ought to have of the other" (Martin, p. 69). Never before had such a great significance been placed on love and companionship in the arrangement of marriage.

Before modernity, it had not been in anyway required or expected that a man's most meaningful and fulfilling relationship be with his wife and vice-versa. Same-sex friendships played a much larger role in society and in the lives of individuals. Moreover, the line between friendship and committed relationship was often vague; therefore, crossing this line was less likely to be considered a deviance, let alone a threat to societal order. But in a culture that sees the nuclear family as the "primary unit" (Greenberg p. 372) and the "building block" (Focus on the Family) of society - where men go to work, women take care of the home, children are socialized and the structure is perpetuated – homosexuality is perceived as a threat to the family, and that which is perceived as a "treat to the family [becomes] a threat to the social order itself" (Greenberg 1988, p. 372).

Homosexuality and Communism

When in 1970, a national survey asked U.S. citizens whether "homosexuality is a social corruption which can cause the downfall of a civilization," 49 percent agreed that yes it is (Greenberg 1988, p. 457). College level history texts of the 1960s attributed the fall of the Roman Empire, medieval Arabia, and other civilizations throughout history to homosexuality (Bullough, 1979). Bullough (1979) furthermore observed that links were being drawn between homosexuality and communism, another national enemy. In the 1950s, members of the "House Un-American Activities Committee tended to lump homosexuality, Communism, and subversion in one category" (Bullough, p, 99). When asked whether homosexuality is a moral or a security issue, Kenneth Wherry – a Nebraskan senator and one of the leaders of the antihomosexual crusade - stated that it is both, because "a man of low morality is a menace in the government" (New York post, 1950; quoted in Bullough p. 100). Many government officials, accused of being 'perverts,' lost their jobs in these crusades against homosexuality in America (Bullough, p. 70, 90-100).

It may be interesting to note, as Greenberg (1988) does, that America is more capitalist-oriented and also more anxious about homosexuality than, for instance, the Netherlands where the "welfare-state system [is] more generous" (p. 476) and where the population is known for its 'tolerance' of homosexuality amongst other things. However, I would not be inclined to draw causal relations directly linking homophobia to capitalism. For a causal relation to be made, one would suspect that the further a society moves away from capitalism – with its free market conditions and competition – the greater the level of acceptance towards homosexual people in that society. In theory, Bullough (1979) describes, Marxist critics claim that homophobia is a product of western capitalist thought, where everything is judged by its productive value so that even sex became "measured by a production principle, with procreation being the chief purpose of sex" (p. 96). Homosexuals thus "undermine the capitalist bourgeois performance principle" (p. 97) and can therefore be expected to face stigmatization in a capitalist society. In practice, however, the stigmatization of homosexuals is not limited to capitalist societies. It is no less common or less severe in communist societies (Bullough, 1979).

Modernization and the Construction of Homosexuality

As the theories suggest, perhaps modernization and capitalism created a problem for the free expression of homosexuality. Meanwhile, another aspect of modernization, namely urbanization, brought an increasing number of these fresh outcasts in contact with each other, allowing them to collectively define, and procure a space for, themselves in modern society.

Urbanization

Dormor (2007) describes the establishment of 'molly' houses – taverns where men were known to socialize and flirt with each other - in late 17th century England, especially in cities such as London. "Those whose affections and perhaps sexual relationships could no longer be concealed within the homosocial world of bedfellows, whose homoerotic desires could find shelter no more under the codes of Christian friendship, found a place to be…with others who were similarly inclined" (p. 82). When homosexual people were beginning to be perceived as a distinct type of people, and were discriminated against based on this distinction, "molly-houses brought together men who shared a common legal risk, making collective response possible" (p. 349). It was the beginning of a new subculture in European society.

Greenberg (1988) explains that, "it was not until the nineteenth century [that] American cities [grew] to the point where homosexual subcultures could form" (p. 346). He theorizes that urbanization – with the increasing densification of the population in particular areas – allowed for the development of 'homosexuality' as a category and marker of identity that created a line of distinction between two types of people: heterosexuals and homosexuals. "As cities grew, urban male homosexual networks grew along with them" (Greenberg, p. 383). Boswell (1980) describes a subculture as "a network of [individuals], conscious of their common difference from the majority and mutually influencing their own and others' perception of the nature of their distinctiveness" (p. 243). For a subculture to develop between people that share a common trait – such as a sexual attraction towards people of the same sex – a significant number of such people must have the opportunity to come in contact with each other, first of all, to discover their similarity. One 'homosexual' in a village of seemingly all 'heterosexuals' is unlike to set himself off from the other villagers and define himself as 'a homosexual' if he does not know there are others like him.

However, urbanization alone is not enough to account for the development a new subculture of homosexuals. It is one thing that more 'homosexual' people were put in contact with each other and allowed to discover that they had something in common, but for them to claim this similarity as a marker of identity – as something that sets them apart from those who do not have it – involves a rather more complex process. What made them so "conscious of their common difference"?

Discrimination Gives Rise to Unification?

The discovery of a shared trait does not automatically give rise to a new subculture. For example, a person who writes with his left hand, rather than his right hand, may soon discover that he is not the only one who does so – yet left-handed people do not (and are not) group(ed) together as a distinct type of people. That is, their deviance from the majority has no social significance (Boswell, 1980). Why then did people that were primarily attracted to those of the same sex need to construct a collective identity? Recall from the section on *Why the Africans became the slaves* in this thesis that African people in the Americas were particularly vulnerable to exploitation because they had not yet developed a sense of shared identity from which to derive power and agency to defend themselves. Unification is very important in the struggle for collective rights to improve the situation for individuals. This can be observed, for example, in the case of initially dissident tribes of natives that unite and developed a pan-culture to defend themselves against colonizers. Thus it can be said that discrimination towards a particular type of people gives rise to the unification of those people – they begin to identity themselves by their shared minority status in order to derive power from this collective, constructed identity.

However, if discrimination gives rise to unification, one can ask: what gave rise to discrimination? One could argue that discrimination against a group of people cannot occur if that social category does not first exist. For instance, Sanday (1981), in her research on the origins of sexual inequality says, "Men and women must be physically as well as conceptually separated in order for men to dominate women" (p. 7). In virtually 'unisex' cultures, such as the Balinese, male dominance does not occur (Sanday, 1981). Likewise, it is conceivable that heterosexual and homosexual needed to be separate categories before the institutionalized discrimination of one 'group' against the other could occur. However, I do not intend to go into a what-came-first-the-chicken-or-the-egg type of discussion. I would propose that, like the development of the concept of race and the discrimination of 'black' people, explored in the previous chapter of this thesis, the construction of homosexuality as a category and the institutionalized discrimination against 'homosexual' people probably developed rather simultaneously and tied in with each other – one strengthening the other. In any case, a biological way of thinking and classifying contributed greatly to the social construction, and individual claiming, of a homosexual identity.

The New Scientific View

Greenberg (1988) states that modern "science was important…for introducing materialist explanations of human behavior" (Greenberg, p. 350). Initially, the new scientific view gave those who experienced discrimination on the bases of their sexuality a starting point for claiming equal rights and legitimacy. Whereas homosexuals may previously have been accused of sodomy – a term that initially covered much more than just *homo*sexual acts but came to be applied to homosexual people in particular (Boswell 1980; Dormor 2007) – they could now argue that it was in their nature, that it was part of their essence and identity, to act this way. Greenberg (1988) gives account of a seventeenth century priest who told a confessor of homosexual love:

"'That is a sin against nature' and was told in reply 'Oh father, but it is very natural to me'" (p. 350).

Douglas (1986; see also the theory chapter of this thesis) said that as labels are invented to identify people that have been grouped together on the bases of a society's classification system, those people may come to claim the label as their identity. Perhaps one good reason for doing this is the sense of validity that comes with the label. Bullough (1979) draws a parallel between the civil rights and the gay liberation movement by saying that "Just as the black movement capitalized on one of the most hidden fears of blacks – being called black – by making the feared word a symbol and proclaiming that black is beautiful, homosexuals have also proclaimed that gay is good" (p. 84). They have accepted the label given to them by society and wear it with pride.

In our society, it seems almost unthinkable that our sexual categories and labels (hetero-, bi-, or homosexual) do not exist everywhere. We assume that there are 'homosexual' people in all societies anywhere in the world - and that they are fundamentally distinct from 'heterosexual' people -because we identify these categories as occurrences of nature with a biological root, just as we perceive the difference between male and female to be essentially biological. We are still in the grips of a bio-medical/scientific world-view. We try to find scientific explanations for, and thus essentialize, human characteristics that are observable and significant in our social world. This is not to say that scientific discoveries concerning essential differences between, for instance, men and women or hetero- and homosexual people are baloney, but their discovery is steered by, and made significant by, the culture in which they are discovered. Parker (2001) notes that "biological reductionists… don't go looking for the gene for 'parental affection'" (p. 334), or other traits which may well have a biological component but do not have any social significance and do not define a person in our culture. Yet scientists look for biological explanations for the observable difference between men and women in our society, because these differences are perceived as significant.

Likewise, there is the ongoing search for the 'gay gene' – an essential part of someone that determines whether that person *is* or *is not* gay – whereas Parker (2001) would claim "there can no more be a 'gene' for homosexuality than there can be a gene for Republicanism" (p. 334) because both are social constructs. Again, this is not to say that one cannot be born with the potential to be exclusively attracted to members of the same sex, but a certain cultural context and culturally constructed categories are required for such a trait to become a salient marker of identity in society. As discussed earlier, for example, in pre-modern England - where same-sex friendships were commonly very intimate and the relationship between husband and wife held less companionate and/or romantic significance – the 'homosexual' could 'get away' with homosexual behavior without being perceived as a different type of person.

The Anthropology of Sexuality

MacCormack (1980) notes that, "By the mid eighteenth century, a well-established bio-medical tradition observed and defined humans, hardening the conceptual division between unique feminine and unique masculine attributes" (p. 21). MacCormack (1980) further describes that Europeans, being a dominant power since colonialism, tend to universalize their bio-medically based gender classifications, becoming 'deaf and blind' to different ways of structuring the world. Ours is the "dominant code," whilst other codes are "muted" (MacCormack, 1980). That is, other systems of structuring the world are perceived as less realistic. For instance, Parker (2001) relates a typical western reaction upon learning about the 'third genders' of other cultures - "Yes, but don't these various groups know that the *berdache*, etc. are *really* men or *really* women" (p. 345) - and explains that, yes, people in these cultures can see the biological differences between male and female, but these are not that important to them and do not necessarily define them.

Parker (2001) explains that, when Western people try to research and understand the sexual acts and values of people in other cultures, they often begin their quest with the assumption that our classification system is natural and, therefore, universal. When in fact there is nothing universal about the "hetero versus homo split" (Parker, p. 316). In his article, *The Myth of the Heterosexual: Anthropology and Sexuality for Classicists*, Parker (2001) explores "the widely differing systems that cultures throughout time and the world have used to classify people and their sexual acts" (p. 313). He explains that 'our' system - which classifies people on the bases of whether or not they (would) engage in sexual activity with someone of the same sex – is comparatively rare in the world and fairly recent in the west.

Parker (2001) makes clear the distinction between *emic* and *etic* categories. Emic categories are those that apply only inside certain cultures. Emic categories "may lump together what another culture keeps rigorously separate" or conversely, "may separate what another considers a distinctive unity" (p. 321). 'Homosexual' is an emic category or label because it cannot simply be applied to any person in any culture who sleeps with people or a person of the same biological sex. It is a category that cannot be translated into another culture but is depended on the context of modern western society, and the way we view sex and sexuality, for its meaning.

For example, the Greeks made a distinction between men that are 'passive' versus men that are 'active' in sexual contact with each other. Where we would label them both as 'homosexual' - and perhaps perceive them as inferior to 'normal,' 'heterosexual' man based on societal and religious prejudices - the Greeks would only see the passive man as inferior whereas the active man would be considered as good and as 'normal' as any other man. Our culture assumes a binary way of thinking about sexuality, "that the only orientation that can exist is either towards people of the same sex or of a different sex" (Parker, p. 324). Whereas another culture's way of thinking about sexual orientation may not consider significant the gender of the people involved, but, for example, the role they play in the sexual act.

Moreover, Parker observes that the terms 'homosexual' and 'heterosexual' cannot be applied in all cultures because not all cultures have the same, binary-oppositions, concept of gender as we do in the Western world. As mentioned earlier, nature simply does not produce all humans as clearly male or female. We perceive it be this way because we have been conditioned to think this way about gender. But other cultures have different systems. Whereas "we base our division of sexual categories on the axis of *same* versus *different* [and] our primary division rests on the gender of the people involved…you cannot ethnocentrically assume the universality of hetero versus homo when you may have more than two choices" (339). Parker (2001) presents a chart (p. 341) in which different cultural systems of classifying gender and sexuality are clarified.

CHART LEGEND		
Sex/Body Type/Biology		Gender/Social
♂ male	△	man
♀ female	○	woman
⚥ hermaphrodite	□	other
	▲	alternative male
	◎	alternative female
	----	has sex with
	⇥	not fully recognized by the culture

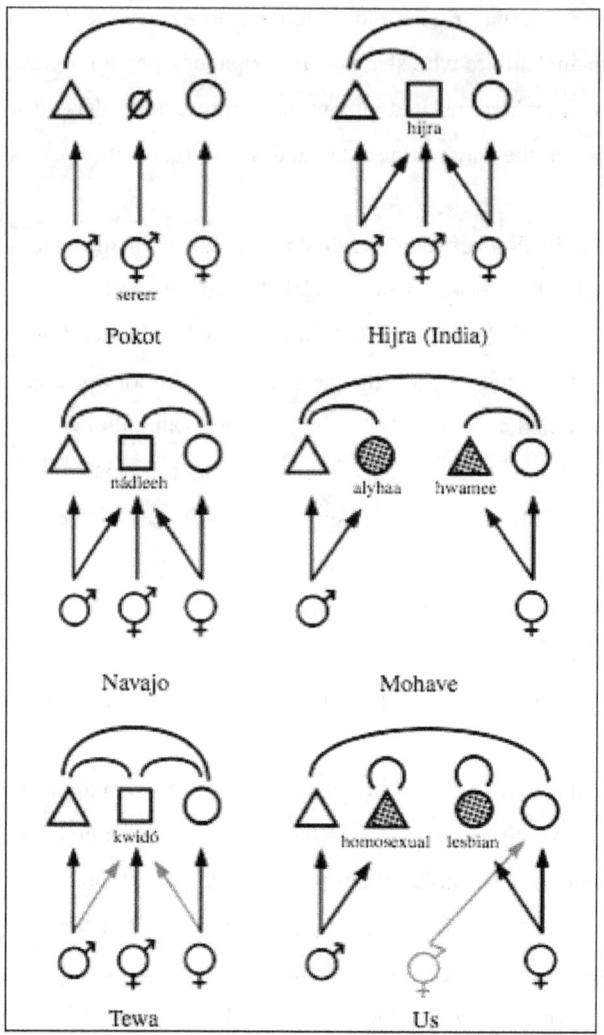

The acceptance of what we would call 'homosexuality' is therefore not a case of one society being more tolerant than another (Greenberg, 1988), but is rather based on different cultural systems of classifying people and structuring society. Likewise, the discrimination towards homosexuals that can be observed in many western societies today, and especially amongst the religious, points not so much towards an inherently intolerant character of these people or groups but is tied in with their structuring system and their paradigm for thinking about gender and sexuality. That is, if the system was different, they would have no bases for their discrimination

– the very category of 'homosexual' might not even have been there to discriminate against in the first place.

Social Change – Moving Towards Equality

Just like race, homosexuality is a social construct. Through societal processes that may be related to modernization, 'homosexuals' came to be grouped as a distinct type of people. And just as 'black' people were perceived as subordinate to 'white' people, 'homosexuals' have been - and by many conservatives in society still are - perceived as inferior to 'heterosexual' people. In the fight for equal rights, homosexuals have compared their plight to that of black people in America.

In the Beginning...

Bullough (1979) and Greenberg (1988) narrate the beginning of the gay liberation movement with an incident occurring on "Friday, June 27, 1969, when the Stonewall Inn, a popular gay men's bar in the Greenwich Village section of New York City was raided by police" (Bullough, p. 63). Such raids were not uncommon and this was not the first time for this particular bar, either. However, on this particular night, the bar man decided he was not going to put up with it any longer; he lost his temper and fought back. The next night, a crowd of supporters gathered near the bar and had a confrontation with the police. "This went on for four more nights before things quieted down, but the gays no longer were content to be as docile as they had been, and ot of the Stonewall riots came the Gay Liberation Front" (Bullough, p. 63). Bullough (1979) further accounts the commemoration of what came to be known as Gay Liberation Day with parades organized in various cities throughout America. Greenberg (1988) also goes on to describe a movement of previously closeted homosexuals suddenly confronting the public with their presence - collaborating and forming liberation groups to organize protests, demonstrations, and parades - after that crucial day in June, 1969.

A parallel can be drawn between this account and the way the beginning of the Civil Rights movement is typically narrated. One individual, who decided he or she would no longer put up with discrimination, gains supporters and the event attracts media attention. Protests become formally organized and turn into a movement. Official groups are established and leaders elected to fuel and organize the movement. For example, accounts of the Civil Rights movement (e.g. Garrow, 1986; Oates, 1982) often begin with Rosa Parks' act of civil disobedience when she refused to give up her seat in a crowded bus so that a white man could sit segregated from black people. The event and proceeding trial gained widespread attention and media coverage and other black people began following her example, leading to the officially organized Montgomery Bus Boycott and the formation of a new association, the Montgomery Improvement Association, of which Martin Luther King was asked to president (Garrow, 1986; Oates, 1982). The end of the story being that the Civil Rights movement became a national campaign which eventually led to equal rights for black people in American society.

The Individual

These narrations account of the impact of individual nonconformity in starting the process of social change, and can be said to provide historical case examples of findings of social psychology experiments on conformity vs. independence (Asch, see Levine, 1999) and obedience vs. disobedience (Milgram, 1965) introduced in the theory chapter of this thesis. Further experiments conducted by Asch (Levine 1999) and Milgram (1965) indicated that one case of nonconformity could liberate others from the pressure to conform. Asch (Levine, 1999) found that "he could increase independence rather dramatically…by having a single confederate dissent from the erroneous majority by giving correct responses" (p. 359). In Milgram's experiment, the amount of subjects obedient to the cruel demands of the experiment also decreased dramatically when they were presented with a civilly disobedient confederate. "The initial definition of the situation…must be abandoned. Only when the original assumption is questioned and a new definition of the situation introduced, does the consequent flow of events give the lie to the assumptions" (Merton, 1957, p. 424).

Applying Merton's quote to the situation of gay rights: one of the 'initial definitions' of homosexuality was that it was a mental disorder. The 'original assumption,' held my mental health professionals, researchers, theologians, and the general population, was that homosexuality was "chosen, abnormal, deviant, and unnatural" (Ontario Consultants on Religious Tolerance 2002, p. 1). In 1957 these beliefs were challenged by a psychological study, conducted by Evelyn Hooker, called *The Adjustment of the Male Overt Homosexual*. Before Hooker's research, homosexuals were rarely the subjects of scientific or psychological study. If they were, the psychiatrists or psychologist conducting the research tended to take a biased test sample of homosexuals who were in prison or in therapy (Ontario Consultants on Religious Tolerance, 2002). "There were simply no scientific data about nonimprisoned, nonpatient homosexuals" (UC Davis website). Evelyn Hooker compared the adjustment of non-clinical homosexual men to that of non-clinical heterosexual men. Other variables between the two groups, such as age and education level, were kept constant. The men were subjected to various personality tests. Hooker than presented these test results to a panel of expert psychologist. These psychologists could not distinguish the test results of the homosexual men from those of the heterosexual men. Nor did they find any pathologies in the test results of the homosexuals. Her pioneer research not only opened up homosexuality as a field of study, greatly impacting the gay rights cause, but also eventually led to the American Psychiatric Association's decision in 1973 to remove homosexuality from its Diagnostic and Statistical Manual of Mental Disorders (DSM). Evelyn Hooker has been referred to as "the Rosa Parks of the gay rights movement" by historian Eric Marcus, quoted in the Los Angeles Times (Oliver, 1996).

New Definitions and Changing Laws

Just as Lincoln's Emancipation Proclamation created the possibility for white Americans to stop seeing black Americans as slaves by definition, so Hooker's findings allowed psychologist and the rest of the population to stop seeing homosexuals as deviant by definition. "'Her work in the 1950s really provided the framework within which the American Psychiatric Association could rethink its viewpoint,' said Dr. Richard A. Isay, clinical professor of psychiatry at the Cornell University Medical College." (Dunlap, 1996). The University of Chicago established the Evelyn Hooker Center for the Mental Health of Gays and Lesbians in her honor. Hooker went on to become president of the National Institute of Mental Health Task Force on Homosexuality. Her panel advocated "a repeal of sodomy laws and better public education about homosexuality" (Dunlap, 1996).

Since the beginning of the gay liberation movement, states have repealed laws that criminalize homosexuality. This has been an important step. Greenberg (1988) reminds the reader that, "The very adoption and enforcement of a law can sway public opinion" (p. 9). Recall also that the same point was argued in the *Changing Attitudes Toward Slavery* section of this thesis. So long as homosexuality was still against the law – or slaveholding, for that matter, was still in accordance with the law – people were unlikely to pull into question their personal opinions about the morality of such actions. It can be said that changing laws and new scientific/psychological definitions of homosexuality have opened up the possibility for individuals in society to adopt more accepting attitudes. However, gay rights are still restricted and, as discussed earlier (see *labeling as dangerous* section), attempts, especially by conservative Christians, to exclude homosexuals from social institutions and nuclear-family life are ongoing.

Churches' Responses

The comparison between the struggle for the rights of black people and that of gay people in American society can be drawn even further back. Just as the Quakers can be said to have been the first organized group to publicly denounce slavery (Peabody & Grinberg, 2007; d'Anjou, 1996; Blackburn, 1988), Bullough (1979) points them out as "the most important" liberal reform group aimed at providing support to out-cast homosexuals as early as the 1940s (p, 68). But just as had been the case with the early abolition of slavery movement, the Quakers were not assertive in gaining power for their cause.

Back to the present, Ontario Consultants on Religious Tolerance (2008) sum up the current situation of the church about homosexuality by saying,

- The more liberal denominations, like the United Church of Christ, have changing their positions on homosexuality, in recent years, to adopt a more inclusive stance.
- Mainline denominations such as the Methodists, Presbyterians and Episcopalians are actively debating the question. A future church schism may result, particularly in the case of the Presbyterian Church (USA), and Episcopal Church. USA.
- More conservative denominations are taking no significant action to change their beliefs and policies at this time.
- Fundamentalist denominations commit significant effort against homosexuality and homosexual rights. For example, the *Southern Baptist Convention* expelled three of their congregations who had conducted a study of homosexuality, had concluded that the denomination's beliefs were invalid, and who welcomed gays and lesbians as members." (p. 1).

In general, Christian churches appear to be moving towards becoming more and more accepting and inclusive of homosexual people. For extensive essays on individual church denominations and their involvement in the debate and policies on homosexuality, visit religioustolerance.org.

Deconstructing Discrimination

Reality

What this thesis has tried to show is that classification systems confer identities. A culture's classification system selects which differences between people become significant and form the lines of distinction that mark one group of people off from another. The process of this differentiation often goes hand in hand with the subordination of one group of people by another. For example, African people were subordinated by Europeans in America and they were classified as a distinct race of black people. Their subordination was then justified because they were this distinct race of people that God had allegedly cursed to slavery. Africans were perceived as 'black' because they were slaves, and slaves because they were black. The reality of race became institutionalized through the system of slavery and reified in the minds of individuals.

This process is more difficult to point out in the case of homosexuality. What can be said is that homosexuality, like race, is a social construct; and homosexuals, like black people in America, have suffered discrimination. Classification systems, which construct categories/identities, are themselves constructed rather than fixed. It can be theorized that society's current classification system that emphasizes and essentializes the distinction between the male and female categories and gender roles, and is therefore threatened by the presence of homosexual people, developed in the process of modernization and the rise of capitalism. Today, strict gender distinctions are perhaps waning as women can do many of the things that were previously only accessible to men in society. Conversely, it is not uncommon for men now-a-days to become more involved in the household, which was previously the women's domain. However, the categories of 'homosexual' vs. 'heterosexual' remain in our minds to structure the way we perceive reality and identify others and ourselves. "Because they give guidance in times of need, metaphors for sexual identities persist long after the circumstances giving rise to them have changed" (Sanday 1981, p. 56). Likewise, African Americans and white Americans are still perceived as distinct identities, even though the institution of slavery, which can be said to have given rise to these categories, has been abolished long ago.

The socially constructed identities have been adopted by the discriminated groups themselves and have often been used powerfully in the struggle for equal rights. Differences (such as race or sexual orientation) by which people discriminate others, or for which people have been discriminated by other, become essentialized. Rather than saying 'we are no different from you,' it can be noted that those who are being discriminated prefer to say 'we cannot help being different.' Rather than being deconstructed, identities are reaffirmed. Not only have individuals adopted the labels that their society has constructed for them, but in their struggle for equal rights they have found it important to wear the label with pride: 'black is beautiful' and 'gay is good.'

Reactions

What reactions can be expected when traditional social structures and beliefs are pulled into question? The answer to this question lies in the analysis of the discourse used by anti-abolitionist or anti-gay rights conservative Christian. Sanday (1981) appropriately observes, "If the whole complex of traditional roles is undermined, people will fight as if they were struggling to hold on to life itself" (p. 163). My conclusion is that discourse of discrimination does not arise from universal, innate, or substantive prejudices but is based on a specific system of classification under threat.

Restructuring

How are discriminatory practices and attitudes ever changed? From the examples and theories provided in this thesis, one can agree with Sanday (1981) that "Things change when tensions are such that without change, things would come apart" (p. 11). Recall the words of Lincoln (1864), "the moment came when I felt that slavery must die that the nation might live," (quoted in Howard 1999, p. 190) and those of Desmond Tutu (2007) that, "the future of Anglicanism depends on upon [a deeper and more open conversation about the issue of homosexuality] taking place" (quoted in Dormor & Morris 2007, p. ix). This thesis has tried to show that individuals can play an important role in creating the social tension required to make change possible. One individual can decide to no longer conform to social practices or established norms that he or she regards as immoral and unjust. This person may gain supporters and a group of individuals can start a movement, organize protests and events, raise awareness for their cause, etc. "The initial definition of a situation…must be abandoned. Only when the original assumption is questioned and a new definition of the situation introduced, does the consequent flow of events give the lie to the assumptions" (Merton 1957, p. 424).

In order to understand discriminating attitudes, I believe it is important to understand the definitions by which people discriminate. What defines someone as 'black' or 'homosexual' in our culture? And how has this been different in other cultures, historically and globally? Investigating these questions will show that the very categories by which we discriminate are social constructs. They are not universal, innate, or natural. While someone may be born with black skin, he or she is not a black person unless others define him as such. And the same argument can be used for the homosexual person.

Nor do I believe our categories and accompanying prejudices are God given. Many conservative Christians used to staunchly believe that the subordination of black people was God ordained. Only after slavery was abolished did this assumption begin to change. "...the church had near unanimity of opinion and then, over time and painfully, changed its mind to almost the exact opposite view" (Rogers 2006, p. 17). Christians, just like all other people, adopt the social categories of their society. But religious people want to perceive things as having been established that way by God. With this thesis I want to show that rather than using bible passages to discriminate against others, Christians should understand the message that, "There is neither Jew nor Greek, slave nor free, male nor female, for you are all one in Christ" (Galatians 3:23). It is people and societies that construct these categories and use them to discriminate.

References

Bem, S. L. (1995). Dismantling gender polarization and compulsory heterosexuality: should we turn the volume down or up? *The Journal of Sex Research, 32*(4). 329-334.

Beyond ExGay: http://www.beyondexgay.com/

Blackburn, R. (1988) *The Overthrow of Colonial Slavery: 1776-1848.* London:Verso.

Black is Beautiful: Rubens to Dumas. (Expedition in the Nieuwe Kerk Amsterdam, 26 July- 26 October, 2008). Zwolle: Waanders Publishers.

Boskin, J (1972). Race relations in seventeenth century America: the problem of the origins of negro slavery. In D. L. Noel (Ed.), *The origins of American slavery and racism* (p. 95-104). Columbus, Ohio: Charles E. Merril Publishing Co.

Boswell, J. (1980). *Christianity, Social Tolerance, and Homosexuality: Gay People in Western Europe from the Beginning of the Christian Era to the Fourteenth Century.* Chicago: University of Chicago Press.

Brienen, R. P. (2006). *Visions of Savage Paradise: Albert Eckhout, Court Painter in Colonial Dutch Brazil.* Amsterdam: Amsterdam University Press.

Bullough, V. L. (1979). *Homosexuality: A History from Ancient Greece to Gay Liberation.* New York: New American Library.

Dabney, R. L. (1867). *A Defense of Virginia (and through her, of the South,) in Recent and Pending Contests Against the Sectional Party.* New York: E. J. Hale & Son.

D'Anjou, L. (1996). *Social Movements and Cultural Change: The First Abolition Campaign Revisited.* New York: Aldine De Gruyter.

De Jong, M. J. (2007). *Icons of Sociology.* Amsterdam: Boom-Academic.

Dormor, D. (2007). "Friends, companions and bedfellows: sexuality and social change." In D. Dormor & J. Morris, (Eds.) *An Acceptable Sacrifice? Homosexuality and the Church.* London:SPCK (p. 74-85)

Dormor, D. & Morris, J. (Eds.). (2007). *An Acceptable Sacrifice? Homosexuality and the Church.* London:SPCK

Douglas, M (1999). *Leviticus as Literature.* New York: Oxford University Press Inc.

Douglas, M (1976). *Reinheid en Gevaar.* (E. Marije, Trans.). Utrecht: Het Spectrum. (Original work published 1966).

Douglas, M. (1986). *How Institutions Think.* New York: Syracuse University Press.

Dunlap, D. W. (1996). Obituary of Evelyn Hooker, 89, Researcher on Homosexuality. *New York Times, November 22, 1996.* Retrieved on April 30, 2009. From: http://psychology.ucdavis.edu/rainbow/html/hooker2.html#biography

Evangelicals Concerned: http://www.ecwr.org/

FOTF Issue Analyst (2008). *Cause for Concern (Pro-Gay Theology): The pro-gay revisionist theology threatens to substantially alter the Christian church and biblical doctrine.* Retrieved 27 April, 2009 from: http://www.focusonthefamily.com/socialissues/sexual_identity/progay_revisionist_theology/cause_for_concern.aspx

FOTF Analyst. (2009). *Focus on the Family Issue Analysis: Overcoming Homosexuality.* http://www.citizenlink.org/FOSI/homosexuality/overcoming/A000009534.cfm# Retrieved: 2 April, 2009.

Franklin, J. H. The Emancipation Proclamation. In J. T. Baker (Ed.). *Abraham Lincoln: The Man and the Myth* (p. 84-87). Orlando, Florida: Harcourt College Publishers.

Furman, R. (1838). *Exposition of The Views of the Baptists, Relative to the Coloured Population in the United States in a Communication to the Governor of South-Carolina (2nd edition).* Charleston: A. E. Miller. Retrieved 17 February 2009. From: http://facweb.furman.edu/~benson/docs/rcd-fmn1.htm

Gay Christian Network: http://www.gaychristian.net/

Greenberg, D. F. (1988). *The Construction of Homosexuality.* Chicago: University of Chicago Press.

Goeke, M. (2009). *How can I love homosexuals and hate homosexuality?* Exodus International – FAQs. Retrieved on 2 April, 2009: From: http://exodus.to/content/view/317/87/

Hare, J. (2007). "Neither male nor female': the case of intersexuality." In D. Dormor & J. Morris, (Eds.) *An Acceptable Sacrifice? Homosexuality and the Church.* London:SPCK (p. 98-112).

Handlin, O., & Handlin, M. F. (1972). The origins of negro slavery. In D. L. Noel (Ed.), *The origins of American slavery and racism* (p. 21-44). Columbus, Ohio: Charles E. Merril Publishing Co.

Jeremiah, D. (2008, March 27th). *Homosexuality more dangerous than terrorism in America.* Retrieved November 7, 2008, from www.tulsabeacon.com/?p=203

LaBarbera, P. (2009a, March 26). *Former Homosexual Comments on George Weber Sex Murder by Young 'Sadomasochist.'* Americans for Truth About Homosexuality. Retrieved: April 2, 2009, From: http://americansfortruth.com/news/former-homosexual-comments-on-george-weber-sex-cruising-murder.html#more-2664

LaBarbera, p. (2009b, March 27). *Former Homosexual DL Foster Says Hook-up Culture that Killed George Weber is Common in Gay World.* Americans for Truth About Homosexuality. Retrieved; April 2, 2009. From: http://americansfortruth.com/news/former-homosexual-dl-foster-says-hook-up-culture-that-killed-george-weber-is-common-in-gay-world.html#more-2668

LaBarbera, P. (2009c, March 24). *Gay Liberation Network Applauds Wright State University's Ban on Christian Bible Group.* Americans For Truth About Homosexuality. Retrieved: 2 April, 2009, From: http://americansfortruth.com/news/gay-liberation-network-applauds-wright-state-universitys-ban-on-christian-bible-group.html#more-2659

LaBarbera, P. (2009d, March 28). *The Agenda: GLBTQ Activist Groups. Promoting perversion pays- professional homosexual activists draw massive salaries.* Americans for Truth About Homosexuality. Retrieved; 2 April, 2009. From: http://americansfortruth.com/issues/the-agenda-glbtq-activist-groups

Lambek, M. (Ed). (2007). *A Reader in the Anthropology of Religion.* Malden, MA: Blackwell Publishing Ltd.

Lincoln, A. (1862). An Address to Free Blacks – August 14, 1862. In J. T. Baker (Ed.). *Abraham Lincoln: The Man and the Myth* (p. 62-63). Orlando, Florida: Harcourt College Publishers.

Lincoln, A. (1837). Statement on Slavery – March 3, 1837. In J. T. Baker (Ed.). *Abraham Lincoln: The Man and the Myth* (p. 58). Orlando, Florida: Harcourt College Publishers.

MacCormack, C. & Strathern, M. (Eds.), (1980). *Nature, Culture, and Gender.* London: Cambridge University Press.

Martin, J. (2007). "Godly conversations: marriage, the companionate life and the Church of England." In D. Dormor & J. Morris, (Eds.) *An Acceptable Sacrifice? Homosexuality and the Church.* London:SPCK (p. 62-74)

McDonagh, E. L. (1976). Attitude change and paradigm shifts: social psychological foundations of the Kuhnian Thesis. *Social Studies of Science*, 6(1 Feb.), p. 51-76.

Merton, R. K. (1957). *Social Theory and Social Structure.* New York: The Free Press.

Morgan, E. S. (1975). *American Slavery, American Freedom: The Ordeal of Colonial Virginia.* New York: W.W. Norton & Company, Inc.

Nash, G. B. (1972). Red, white, and black: the origins of racism in colonial America. In D. L. Noel (Ed.), *The origins of American slavery and racism* (p. 131-152). Columbus, Ohio: Charles E. Merril Publishing Co.

Noel, D. L. (1972a). *The Origins of American Slavery and Racism.* Columbus, Ohio: Charles E. Merril Publishing Co.

Noel, D. L. (1972b). Slavery and the rise of racism. In D. L. Noel (Ed.), *The origins of American slavery and racism* (p. 153-174). Columbus, Ohio: Charles E. Merril Publishing Co.

Noel, D. L. (1972c). A theory of the origin of ethnic stratification. In D. L. Noel (Ed.), *The origins of American slavery and racism* (p. 106-127). Columbus, Ohio: Charles E. Merril Publishing Co.

Ontario Consultant on Religious Tolerance (2002). "History of the gay liberation movement and the 'homosexual agenda'" (2002, July 23). Retrieved April 30, 2009, from: http://www.religioustolerance.org/hom_agen.htm

Ontario Consultants on Religious Tolerance (2006). "Religions changing their beliefs" (2006, May 29). Retrieved on April 28, 2009, from: http://www.religioustolerance.org/chgintro.htm

Ontario Consultants on Religious Tolerance (2008). "Policies of 47 Different Christian Faith groups about homosexuality" (2008, Aug. 4). Retrieved April 30, 2009. From: http://www.religioustolerance.org/hom_chur2.htm

Oliver, M. (1996). Evelyn Hooker: her study fueled gay liberation. *Los Angeles Times*. November 22, p. 32. Retrieved 30 April 30, 2009 From: http://psychology.ucdavis.edu/rainbow/html/hooker2.html#biography

Parker, H. N. (2001). The myth of the heterosexual: anthropology and sexuality for classicists. *Arethusa 34*. 313-362. John Hopkins University Press.

Peabody, S. & Grinberg, K. (2007). *Slavery, Freedom, and the Law in the Atlantic World: A Brief History with Documents*. Boston: Bedford/St. Martin's

Price, C. H. (2009). *Issue analysis: what about intersexuality?* Focus on the Family. Retrieved, April 02, 2009, from http://www.citizenlink.org/FOSI/homosexuality/concerns/A000007500.cfm

Sanday, P. R. (1981). *Female Power and Male Dominance: On the Origins of Sexual Inequality*. London: Cambridge University Press.

Stark, R (2004). *For the Glory of God: How monotheism led to Reformations, Science, Witch-hunts, and the End of Slavery*. Princeton University Press: Quoted in Keller, T. (2008). *The Reason for God*. New York: Penguin Group (USA) Inc.

Tignor, Adelman, Aron, Brown, Elman, Kotkin, Lui, Merchand, Pittman, Prakash, Shaw, & Tsin, (2008). *Worlds Together, Worlds Apart: A History of the World* (2nd ed.). New York: W.W. Norton & Company.

Tise, L. E. (1987). *Proslavery; A History of the Defense of Slavery in America, 1701-1840*. Athens, Georgia: University of Georgia Press.

UC Davis Website. Biography sketch – Evelyn Hooker, Ph.D. September 2, 1907- November 18, 1996. (Adapted from the *American Psychologist, 1992, 47*, 499-501). Retrieved April 30, 2009. From: http://psychology.ucdavis.edu/rainbow/html/hooker2.html#biography

Wesley, J. (1774). *Thoughts Upon Slavery*. Retrieved 17 February 2009. From: http://gbgm-umc.org/umw/wesley/thoughtsuponslavery.stm

Young, K. & Nathanson, P. "Marriage-a-la-mode: Answering Advocates of Gay Marriage." *Paper presented at Emory University, Atlanta, GA* (May 14, 2003). Retrieved: 20 April, 2009 from: http://catholiceducation.org/articles/sexuality/ho0064.html